LET GO
WITHOUT LOSING YOURSELF

HOW TO RELEASE THE PAST,
RECLAIM YOUR ENERGY,
AND FINALLY MOVE FORWARD

AMELIA OLIVER-LILLY

LET GO WITHOUT LOSING YOURSELF

First edition
Paperback and eBook

Cover and interior design by Big Fat Web
Published by Upload Makers Publishing

CONTENTS

INTRODUCTION
THE WEIGHT YOU'VE BEEN CARRYING

Some things don't stay in the past.

They don't always show up as memories or obvious pain. They don't arrive with urgency or drama.

More often, they exist quietly, woven into how you hesitate before responding, how you brace emotionally, even when nothing is wrong, how calm can feel unfamiliar or temporary.

You may not think about what happened very often. You may not talk about it at all. You might even say, honestly, that you've moved on.

And yet, something still feels unresolved.

Not loud enough to disrupt your life. Not distant enough to release.

Just present enough to shape how you live.

This book is for people who aren't falling apart but are quietly carrying something that no longer belongs in the center of their lives.

When Functioning Isn't the Same as Being Free

Many people assume that if they're functioning well, the past must no longer matter.

They're productive. Capable. Emotionally aware. They show up for work, for relationships, for responsibilities. They've adapted.

But emotional weight doesn't always announce itself as distress.

Sometimes it shows up as:

- Overthinking that feels responsible
- Caution that feels wise
- Independence that feels strong
- Emotional distance that feels calm
- A sense of always being "a little guarded"

These patterns aren't failures.

They're signs that your system learned how to survive something that mattered.

The problem isn't that you adapted.

The problem is that those adaptations stayed in place long after they were needed.

How This Often Feels in Real Life

You might notice it when:

- You replay conversations long after they end
- You prepare explanations you never give
- You struggle to fully relax, even during good moments
- You feel tired in ways that rest doesn't fix
- You hesitate before wanting things fully

None of this means you're broken. These patterns mean your system learned something important and never updated.

Why Letting Go Is So Often Misunderstood

You've probably been told, directly or indirectly, that letting go should be simple by now.

- That time heals
- That insight should be enough
- That forgiveness brings peace

And when those things don't work, people often assume they're doing something wrong.

But letting go isn't a single decision. It's a process that involves your nervous system, your identity, and your sense of safety, not just your understanding.

You don't let go by convincing yourself something shouldn't matter anymore.

You let go when your system learns that it no longer *has to*.

What Letting Go Means in This Book

This isn't a book about erasing your past.

It's not about pretending something didn't hurt. It's not about positivity, spiritual bypassing, or emotional shortcuts.

And it's not about becoming someone new.

Letting go, as it's used here, means:

- The past stops being consulted before decisions
- Old experiences stop defining your reactions
- Emotional charge softens without denial
- You keep the wisdom, but release the weight

Nothing is minimized. Nothing is dismissed. What changes is proximity.

Why Part of You May Resist Letting Go

For many people, letting go doesn't just feel difficult, it feels risky.

Because the past didn't only hurt you.

It also:

- Explained who you became
- Justified your caution
- Protected you from repeating mistakes
- Gave meaning to your growth

Letting go can feel like losing protection, identity, or proof that what you endured mattered.

This book doesn't ask you to abandon those things.

It shows you how to separate meaning from weight, so you don't have to keep carrying pain to preserve truth.

What This Book Will Not Ask of You

This book won't ask you to:

- Forgive before you're ready
- Seek closure from people who can't provide it
- Reopen old wounds to "process" them again
- Relive what already took enough from you
- Perform healing correctly

There is no emotional standard you need to meet here.

No timeline.
No finish line.
No requirement to feel a certain way by the end.

What This Book Will Help You Do

Over the chapters ahead, you'll learn how to:

- Understand why the past still has influence
- Release rumination without suppressing emotion
- Stop waiting for closure that may never come
- Redefine forgiveness without self-betrayal
- Live forward without reopening old wounds
- Rebuild trust in yourself after survival
- Become someone who isn't defined by what hurt them

This isn't a book you rush through.

It's one you move through at your own pace, allowing ideas to settle instead of forcing insight.

How to Read This Book (Gently)

You don't need to read this book linearly.

You don't need to agree with everything immediately.

You don't need to apply everything at once.

Some chapters will feel like they describe you precisely. Others may feel distant, for now.

That's normal.

Healing is contextual. What resonates depends on where you are, not on what you've missed.

A Note About Progress

Progress in this work rarely looks dramatic.

More often, it looks like:

- Catching yourself sooner
- Feeling less urgency
- Recovering more quickly
- Staying present more easily

These aren't small things.

They are signs that your system is learning something new.

You're Not Behind

If you've been carrying something for a long time, you may feel behind, like you should be further along, calmer, more resolved.

But healing isn't linear, and it's not competitive.

The fact that you're here doesn't mean you failed to let go earlier.

It means you're ready to relate to the past differently *now*.

That readiness matters more than timing.

One Last Thing Before You Begin

- You don't need to be sure this will work.

- You don't need to believe letting go is possible.

- You don't need to want it perfectly.

All you need is a willingness to stop carrying what already taught you what it could.

Nothing in this book asks you to lose yourself. If anything, it's designed to help you return to the parts of you that stepped back while you were surviving.

When you're ready, begin.

Not to fix yourself.

But to put something down.

CHAPTER 1

THE PAST DOESN'T HURT YOU: THE GRIP DOES

The past doesn't usually announce itself. It doesn't arrive as a memory you consciously revisit or a story you intentionally replay.

More often, it shows up quietly, woven into how you hesitate before responding, how you scan conversations for tone, how you brace emotionally even when nothing is wrong.

You may not think about what happened very often. You may not talk about it at all. You might even believe, truthfully, that you've moved on.

And yet, something from before still seems to influence how much of your life you allow yourself to inhabit.

This is one of the most confusing aspects of emotional pain: the event itself may be long over, but its impact feels oddly current. Not sharp enough to demand attention. Not distant enough to disappear. Just present enough to shape your reactions.

Most people assume this means they haven't healed properly. That if the past still has influence, they must be doing something wrong.

But that interpretation misses the truth.

The past doesn't hurt you anymore.

The *grip* it still has on you does.

How the Past Becomes Something You Carry

When something emotionally destabilizing happens, whether it was sudden or slow, dramatic or subtle, your system adapts.

That adaptation isn't a failure. It's intelligence.

You become more alert. More cautious. More aware of patterns, tone, timing, and risk. You learn what to avoid, what to expect, and what not to assume again.

At the time, these shifts help you survive.

The problem isn't that your system adapted. The problem is that it never received a clear signal that it could stop.

Life moves forward. Circumstances change. Time passes. But your nervous system doesn't automatically recalibrate just because years go by. It continues to operate as if the original conditions might return.

What once protected you begins to quietly limit you.

How the Grip Shows Up When You're "Doing Fine"

The grip of the past is subtle, which is why it's often misinterpreted. It doesn't always show up as sadness, anger, or obvious distress. In fact, many people carrying the grip are highly functional, emotionally articulate, and outwardly stable.

The grip often looks like:

- Overthinking conversations after they end
- Feeling emotionally tired without a clear reason
- Hesitating before committing, even to things you want
- Struggling to trust calm or ease
- Feeling like you're always "a little behind" in life
- Keeping parts of yourself slightly held back

None of these mean you're broken.

They mean your system learned something important, and never updated.

The Hidden Ways You Keep Holding On (Without Realizing It)

The grip of the past isn't always emotional. Often, it's procedural.

You can be doing fine and still be running old instructions.

Not instructions you consciously chose, but ones you absorbed in the aftermath of whatever happened. The mind and body do this automatically. They create small rules that keep you oriented, protected, and ready.

The problem is that these rules rarely announce themselves as rules. They feel like personality. They feel like being responsible. They feel like being careful in a way you can justify.

But when you look closely, many of them are simply habits of holding on.

Here are a few of the most common ones.

You run "prevention rituals."

A prevention ritual is anything you do to avoid feeling caught off guard. It might look like checking your phone more than you need to, not because you're addicted to it, but because silence feels like a setup.

It might look like reading the same messages over and over to make sure your tone was right. It might look like over-preparing before conversations, appointments, or commitments that aren't actually high stakes.

These rituals don't feel like fear. They feel like competence.

But the underlying message is, *I must stay ahead of discomfort.*

If your nervous system learned that being surprised led to pain, it will try to eliminate surprise entirely. That isn't a moral failure. It's a protective strategy that simply stayed active too long.

You keep a mental "case file."

A case file is the quiet storage system where you keep evidence. Evidence that you were right to leave. Evidence that you were wronged. Evidence that you were not imagining it. Evidence that you should never go back.

This evidence is real. Your mind isn't fabricating it.

But sometimes the case file isn't for you. It's for an imaginary future moment when you will need to defend your experience to someone who never truly understood it.

You might notice the case file activates when you feel doubted, dismissed, or misunderstood in your current life. The past becomes your proof. Your system reaches for it because it still believes you might need to justify yourself.

Letting go doesn't ask you to deny what happened.

It asks you to notice when you're still living as if you're on trial.

You rehearse "repair."

Repair rehearsal is the habit of preparing for a conflict that hasn't happened yet.

You practice how you will explain. You practice how you will stay calm. You practice how you will not be misread. You practice how you will defend your boundaries without sounding harsh.

From the outside, this looks like overthinking. From the inside, it often feels like maturity.

But constant repair rehearsal can be a sign that your system expects relationships to require ongoing management to stay safe.

That expectation doesn't mean you're pessimistic. It means you were trained by experience.

The grip loosens when you start living as if you're allowed to be understood without perfect wording.

You shrink to stay safe.

This one is subtle because it often feels like humility.

You downplay what you want. You delay asking. You soften your preferences. You stop sharing ideas until you're sure they will be received well. You keep your happiness quiet, your excitement controlled, your needs carefully measured.

Not because you're incapable of taking up space, but because taking up space once had consequences.

Sometimes the grip isn't pain. It's self-editing.

Letting go includes allowing yourself to expand again, even if it feels unfamiliar at first.

You keep the past "reachable."

This is one of the most overlooked forms of holding on.

The past becomes reachable when you keep doors cracked open, not necessarily in the external sense, but internally.

You might:

- Keep re-reading old messages
- Keep revisiting old places online
- Keep checking whether someone has changed
- Keep hoping you will feel differently if you find one more piece of information

Even if you dislike doing it, part of you still believes something could shift if you stay close enough.

The grip is strengthened by access.

Not access to the person, but access to the emotional proximity.

This is why one of the most practical forms of letting go is reducing reachability. Less checking. Less revisiting. Less re-entry.

Not because you're punishing yourself, but because you're teaching your system that you live here now.

Why these patterns are hard to stop

If you have been carrying the past for a long time, these habits may feel necessary.

Because they do something for you.

They help you avoid regret. They help you avoid repetition. They help you avoid humiliation. They help you avoid feeling naive.

They also help you avoid a specific kind of discomfort, which is the discomfort of not monitoring.

When you stop monitoring, you may feel exposed at first. Not because you're unsafe, but because you're used to being braced.

That feeling can be misread as intuition. But often it's simply withdrawal from vigilance.

Your system is adjusting to a new baseline.

A small practice that loosens the grip without force

When you notice one of these habits, try this sequence. It's intentionally simple.

- **Name what is happening.**
  Not with criticism, but with accuracy.

  "This is a prevention ritual."
  "This is repair rehearsal."
  "This is my case file."

- **Ask what it's trying to prevent.**
  Don't overanalyze. One sentence is enough.

  "It's trying to prevent being blindsided."
  "It's trying to prevent being misunderstood."
  "It's trying to prevent me from feeling powerless."

- **Offer your system a present-time alternative.**
  This is where the update happens.

  "I can respond if something comes up."
  "I don't need to pre-defend my reality."
  "I can handle discomfort without returning to the past."

This doesn't erase the habit immediately. It changes the relationship.

Instead of being inside the habit, you're now witnessing it. And witnessing creates distance. Distance weakens the grip.

What you're building instead

As these habits soften, you're not becoming careless.

You're becoming less governed. Governed by old rules. Old expectations. Old emergencies that no longer exist.

The goal isn't to eliminate every backward glance. It's to stop living as if backward glances are required for safety.

You will still have memory. You will still have discernment.

What you will have less of is the constant sense that you must keep something active to be okay.

That is what freedom begins to feel like.

Not dramatic relief. Just fewer internal tasks.

More space for your actual life.

What the Grip Is *Not*

This matters.

The grip is not:

- A refusal to move on
- An inability to forgive
- A lack of insight
- Emotional immaturity

You can understand what happened and still feel affected by it.

Insight alone doesn't release the grip, because the grip doesn't live in understanding.

It lives in **expectation**.

The Past Only Has Power Where It's Still Being Consulted

This is one of the most important ideas in the entire book.

The past continues to hurt you only where it's still being used as a reference point.

Where it still answers questions like:

- *Is this safe?*
- *Can I trust this?*
- *What does this mean about me?*
- *How should I protect myself here?*

Every time the past answers those questions, it reinforces its authority.

This isn't something you do on purpose. It's automatic. Your system learned that the past contains important information, so it keeps checking back.

Letting go doesn't mean refusing to look at the past.

It means stopping the habit of consulting it.

Why Understanding What Happened Wasn't Enough

Many people try to heal through explanation.

They analyze what happened. They name patterns. They understand the dynamics. They can articulate exactly why things unfolded the way they did.

And yet, the grip remains.

This can be deeply frustrating. It leads people to believe they haven't found the *right* explanation yet.

But the grip isn't intellectual.

You can *know* something is over and still *react* as if it's ongoing.

Because the body doesn't respond to explanation. It responds to safety.

Letting go isn't about better understanding the past. It's about updating the present.

The Part of You That Doesn't Want to Let Go

Here's something rarely acknowledged:

Part of you believes holding on is necessary.

Not because you enjoy pain, but because the past has been doing important work.

It has:

- Justified your caution
- Explained your boundaries
- Validated your hurt
- Protected you from repeating mistakes

Letting go can feel like removing armor before you're sure the environment is safe.

That resistance doesn't mean you're stuck. It means you're loyal, to survival.

Common Inner Dialogues at This Stage

You may recognize some of these thoughts:

- *If I let this go, I might miss something important.*
- *If I soften, I could get hurt again.*
- *If I stop thinking about it, it might happen again.*
- *This pain taught me something… I can't just drop it.*

These thoughts aren't irrational. They come from a system that learned vigilance equals safety.

Letting go requires a different kind of safety, one that comes from trust in your ability to respond, not prevent.

When the Past Becomes an Identity

Over time, the past can become more than something that happened. It can become a reference point for who you are.

You may unconsciously define yourself as:

- The one who endured
- The one who learned the hard way
- The one who can't afford to be naive
- The one who had to grow up early

These identities are understandable. They reflect real experience.

But when identity is anchored to pain, moving forward can feel like erasing yourself.

This is why letting go can feel like loss, not relief.

Remembering vs. Reliving

Letting go doesn't mean forgetting.

Forgetting is passive and unreliable.

Letting go is active and intentional.

You can remember what happened without re-entering it. You can honor your story without letting it direct your future.

The problem isn't memory.

It's **re-engagement.**

Each time you step back into the past emotionally, analyzing, replaying, defending, you reinforce the grip.

Letting go begins when you stop stepping back in.

What Distance Actually Looks Like

Distance doesn't look like indifference.

It looks like:

- Noticing a memory without following it
- Feeling something old without reopening the story
- Choosing not to analyze what already taught you enough

Imagine placing the past on a shelf a few feet away.

You're not throwing it out. You're not denying it.

You're simply not holding it against your chest anymore.

This teaches your system that proximity is optional.

Why This Can Feel Uncomfortable at First

Creating distance can initially feel wrong.

You may feel:

- Guilty
- Detached
- Unfaithful to your experience
- Afraid something important will be lost

That discomfort isn't a sign you're doing something incorrectly. It's a sign you're doing something *new*.

Your system learned closeness. It's now learning choice.

What Letting Go Actually Changes

Letting go doesn't erase the past.

It changes its authority.

The past stops driving. You start choosing.

And that shift doesn't happen all at once. It happens in small moments, each time you notice the pull and choose not to follow.

When Letting Go Feels Like Betrayal

Some people hesitate to let go because it feels like betrayal.

Betrayal of:

- What you went through
- The version of you that survived
- The truth of what happened

But honoring your experience doesn't require carrying it forever.

You can acknowledge that something mattered *and* decide it no longer gets to shape your life.

Those two things aren't opposites.

A Grounded Question That Changes the Process

Instead of asking:
Why did this happen to me?

Try asking:
What no longer needs to come with me?

This question doesn't demand explanation.

It invites discernment.

Not every lesson needs to be carried forward. Not every adaptation is still useful.

Letting go is sorting, not erasing.

What Freedom Actually Looks Like

Freedom doesn't mean the past never comes up.

It means when it does, it doesn't take you with it.

You stay here.
In your body.
In your life.
In your choices.

That's not repression.

That's presence.

You Don't Have to Be "Over It" to Be Free

You don't need emotional neutrality.
You don't need perfect closure.
You don't need to feel indifferent.

You can still care, and be free.

The goal isn't to stop feeling. The goal is to stop organizing your life around what already happened.

What This Chapter Asks of You

Not perfection.
Not silence.
Not emotional detachment.

Just this:
When the past appears, you don't have to follow.

That single choice, repeated gently over time, is how the grip loosens. And once the grip loosens, something else becomes possible.

You don't just survive your life.

You live it.

CHAPTER 2

WHY YOUR MIND KEEPS GOING BACK: EVEN WHEN YOU WANT PEACE

It often happens when you least expect it.

You're not upset. You're not intentionally thinking about the past. You might even be enjoying yourself, until a thought drifts in without warning. A conversation from years ago. A decision you still quietly question. A version of yourself you thought you'd outgrown.

Suddenly, your attention shifts.

You're no longer fully here. Not because you want to be somewhere else, but because something old has pulled you backward.

This is one of the most frustrating parts of letting go.

You're not clinging. You're not searching. And yet, your mind keeps returning to the same material, as if it hasn't finished with you.

You may have told yourself you're tired of thinking about it. You may have tried to redirect your attention, distract yourself, or reason your way out of it.

And still, it comes back.

This doesn't mean you're weak. It doesn't mean you're obsessed. It doesn't mean you've failed to heal.

It means your mind learned something important, and hasn't been told it can stop checking.

Wanting Peace Isn't the Same as Knowing How to Sustain It

Most people want peace. What they don't realize is that peace isn't the mind's primary goal.

Safety is.

Your mind isn't designed to prioritize calm, ease, or contentment. It's designed to prevent harm. When those goals conflict, safety always wins, even if it comes at the expense of peace.

If something in your past felt unresolved, unpredictable, or emotionally destabilizing, your system marked it as *relevant*. Relevant experiences don't get archived automatically. They stay active, waiting for resolution.

So even when life improves, your mind keeps scanning backward, not because it prefers pain, but because it never received a clear signal that the threat has passed.

What This Looks Like in Everyday Life

This backward pull doesn't usually feel dramatic. It often shows up in subtle, socially acceptable ways.

You might notice:

- Replaying conversations to see if you missed something
- Mentally rehearsing things you wish you'd said
- Revisiting decisions to check whether they doomed you
- Feeling restless in quiet moments
- Struggling to stay present without effort

These aren't habits of obsession.

They're habits of vigilance.

Your mind learned that reflection was protective. Looking back felt like the only way to prevent future pain.

Reflection vs. Rumination: Why the Difference Matters

From the inside, reflection and rumination feel almost identical.

Both involve thinking about the past.
Both feel purposeful.
Both can masquerade as growth.

The difference lies in the outcome.

Reflection leads to clarity, and then completion.
Rumination leads to exhaustion, and then repetition.

Reflection asks, *What can I learn?*
Rumination asks, *How do I make sure this never happens again?*

One ends.
The other loops.

Your mind doesn't ruminate because it enjoys suffering. It ruminates because it believes something is still unresolved.

As long as something feels unfinished, your system keeps it open, like a browser tab you never quite close.

Why Your Mind Reopens Old Tabs (And How to Close Them Gently)

A lot of what we call overthinking is actually an attempt to complete something. Your mind isn't just wandering. It's circling.

It returns to the same conversations, the same decisions, the same moments where something felt unclear or unsafe, because it's trying to reach an endpoint it never got.

This is why rumination often feels like it has a purpose.

It's not random. It's repetitive because it's looking for a specific kind of finish.

But here's the catch.

Many experiences cannot be finished in the way the mind wants. They can only be finished in the way your system allows.

The mind loves "clean endings"

Clean endings have certain qualities. They include:

- Clear cause and effect
- Clear responsibility
- Clear meaning
- Clear next steps
- Clear emotional resolution

When you don't get these qualities, the brain keeps the file open. Not because you're weak, but because it doesn't know where to put the experience.

An unfinished experience stays close.
It stays available.
It keeps interrupting.

This is especially true when the experience involved confusion, contradiction, or emotional whiplash.

If you were told one thing and shown another, your mind will keep revisiting the inconsistency, trying to make it coherent.

Coherence is safety.
So, your brain tries again.
And again.

Why "one more thought" feels necessary

There's a specific feeling inside rumination that makes it hard to stop.

It's the feeling that you're almost there.

Almost to clarity. Almost to peace. Almost to the final insight that will make everything click.

This is why you can spend hours thinking and still feel unfinished. Each loop creates a tiny sense of momentum, but not completion.

Rumination gives motion without arrival.

If you're stuck in a loop, ask yourself this:

What does my mind believe will happen if I stop thinking about this?

Common answers include:

- I will miss something important
- I will repeat it
- I will lose the lesson
- I will be unprepared
- I will be unsafe

These aren't dramatic fears. They are quiet assumptions.

And assumptions can be updated.

The difference between closing a loop and solving a story

Many people try to solve their rumination. They look for the perfect explanation. But rumination is rarely solved. It's closed.

Closing is different from solving.

Solving says, I need the answer. Closing says, I'm done paying for this with my attention.

You can close a loop even when you still don't like what happened. You can close a loop even when you still disagree with the ending.

Closure here isn't approval. It's disengagement.

A practical way to close a loop in real time

When you notice you're back in the same thought pattern, try this three-part response. Keep it short. The point is repetition, not intensity.

Label the loop.
"This is the same loop."
"This is the replay."
"This is my mind trying to finish it."

Name what the loop is seeking.
Usually it's one of these: certainty, fairness, reassurance, control.
"This is seeking certainty."
"This is seeking fairness."
"This is seeking reassurance."

Offer a closing statement.
A closing statement isn't an argument. It's a boundary.
"There is no new information here."
"I don't need to solve this to live today."
"I can tolerate not knowing."
"I choose to be here now."

At first, this can feel too simple to work.

But the mind doesn't stop looping because you explain more. It stops looping when it learns the loop doesn't get rewarded with more engagement.

This is behavioral, not intellectual.

Each time you close it gently, you teach your brain a new exit.

Why redirection works better than suppression

Suppression is saying, stop.
Redirection is saying, this way.

Suppression creates tension. It often increases the sense that the thought is dangerous or urgent.

Redirection is different. You acknowledge the thought, then you anchor somewhere else.

A good anchor is something your nervous system can register immediately.

Try one of these:

- Feel your feet in your shoes
- Notice five objects in the room
- Take one slow breath and count the exhale
- Put your hand on your chest and feel the rise and fall
- Name the date and where you are

These actions aren't spiritual. They are orienting.

They tell your system, we are here.

The past isn't happening.

When the loop returns, you're not back at the beginning

One of the biggest mistakes people make is interpreting the return of rumination as failure.

But loops return for predictable reasons.

They return when you're:

- Tired
- Lonely
- Under pressure
- In transition
- Facing uncertainty
- Near something that resembles the old situation

A loop returning isn't proof that you haven't healed. It's proof that your mind uses looping as a coping strategy.

What matters isn't whether it shows up. What matters is whether you treat it like an emergency.

Progress looks like noticing sooner. Closing faster. Returning more easily.

A reframe that reduces the grip immediately

Instead of asking:
Why am I still thinking about this?

Try:
What is my mind trying to protect me from right now?

This shifts you out of self-criticism and into clarity.

Sometimes the answer has nothing to do with the original event. Your mind may be using the past as a familiar distraction from a present discomfort.

A hard decision. A vulnerable conversation. A new beginning.

In those moments, the mind chooses old pain because it's known.

The goal isn't to shame the mind for doing this. The goal is to bring it back to the present gently, and then address what is actually here.

A simple boundary with your own mind

You can treat your mind like a well-meaning but anxious helper.

It offers you the same file again and again.
You don't need to yell at it.
You just need to respond consistently.

Try this internal boundary:
"Thank you. I understand why you're bringing this up. We aren't working on that right now."

Then choose a next step that is small and real.

Drink water. Take a shower. Answer one email. Walk around the block. Return to the page you were reading.

This is how loops lose their hold.

Not by being defeated. By being outgrown.

Your Mind Isn't Broken: It's Waiting for an Update

This is where self-judgment often enters.

People assume their mind is malfunctioning:

- *Why can't I stop thinking about this?*
- *What's wrong with me?*
- *Why am I still here?*

But your mind isn't broken. It's outdated.

It's operating with information from a different version of you.

At the time of the original experience, you may have lacked:

- Emotional support
- Power
- Perspective
- Boundaries
- Self-trust

Your mind learned strategies based on those conditions.

What it hasn't fully integrated yet is this:
You're not that person anymore.

Without a conscious update, your system keeps replaying old material, trying to protect a version of you that no longer exists.

Why "Just Stop Thinking About It" Never Works

When a thought arises and you try to shut it down, your mind interprets that as danger.

The message it receives is:
This is important, and we're not allowed to look at it.

So, it tries harder.

Suppression increases urgency. Resistance strengthens relevance. This is why mental control strategies backfire. You can't bully a protective system into peace.

Letting go requires cooperation, not domination.

The Quiet Contract You Didn't Know You Made

At some point, your mind made an unspoken agreement with the past:

If I keep revisiting this, I can keep you safe.

Every replay is an attempt to:

- Prevent repetition
- Assign meaning
- Create certainty
- Restore control

The mind isn't trying to punish you. It's trying to ensure competence. The problem is that competence built on fear doesn't age well.

Common Inner Dialogues at This Stage

You may recognize some of these thoughts:

- *If I understand this fully, can I finally move on?*
- *I just need one more insight*
- *What if I'm missing something important?*
- *I don't want to repeat this*

These aren't signs you're stuck. They're signs your system hasn't been told it's safe to disengage.

Why Busyness Only Delays the Loop

Many people cope by staying busy. They work more. Scroll more. Stay stimulated. Stay useful. Stay distracted.

And it works, for a while.

But when things slow down, the mind returns to what still feels unfinished. That's why peace can feel fragile. It exists only when you're occupied.

Busyness doesn't resolve loops. It postpones them. True relief comes from closing loops, not outrunning them.

Closing Loops Without Answers

Here's the difficult truth:
Some loops don't close with answers.

No explanation will arrive.
No apology will come.
No clarity will appear retroactively.

If your mind requires answers to release, it will stay stuck indefinitely.

Instead of asking:
How do I solve this?

Try asking:
How do I disengage from this?

That shift changes everything.

A Different Way to Respond When the Past Appears

When a memory resurfaces, most people automatically engage with it.

They analyze.
They replay.
They argue internally.

Try something different.

When the thought arises, ask:
Is this thought asking for insight, or reassurance?

Most of the time, it's reassurance.

Your system is checking whether you're safe *now*.

Respond briefly, internally:

- *That's over.*
- *I'm not there anymore.*
- *I can handle myself now.*

You're not debating the memory.
You're orienting yourself to the present.

That's how nervous systems learn.

Updating Meaning Without Rewriting History

You don't need to change what happened.
You need to change what it means *now*.

At the time, the experience may have meant:

- *I can't trust myself.*
- *I'm not safe.*
- *I need to stay guarded.*

Those meanings were contextually accurate then.
But meaning isn't permanent.

Letting go involves updating context:

- *I didn't have the tools then.*
- *I do now.*
- *That chapter is closed.*

This isn't denial. It's recalibration.

When the Past Keeps Asking for Proof

Sometimes the mind revisits the past not to understand it, but
to test you.

Have you learned enough?
Are you different now?
Will you make the same mistake again?

These questions aren't answered intellectually.
They're answered through living.

Each time you:

- Respond differently
- Set a boundary
- Choose yourself
- Stay present

Your system takes note.

It doesn't need proof all at once. It just needs consistency.

Giving Yourself Permission to Stop Reviewing

There's a powerful moment in letting go when you realize: *I've thought about this enough.*

You're allowed to say:

- *There's nothing new here.*
- *This no longer needs my attention.*
- *I choose peace over analysis.*

This isn't avoidance. It's discernment.

You don't owe the past endless engagement.

What Peace Actually Feels Like at First

Peace doesn't arrive as silence. It arrives as less urgency.

The thought still appears, but it doesn't hook you.
The memory surfaces, but it doesn't pull you under.
The feeling arises, but it passes more quickly.

This stage is easy to miss if you're waiting for dramatic relief.

But it's real. And it's how peace begins.

Learning to Stay Without Following

One of the most important skills you'll develop is staying present without following your thoughts backward.

You don't suppress them.
You don't argue with them.
You don't engage them.

You notice.
You acknowledge.
You return.

This isn't indifference. It's leadership.

You're teaching your mind that not every thought requires participation.

Why This Takes Practice

Your mind *learned* to revisit the past through repetition.
It will *unlearn* that pattern the same way.

There will be days when old loops return. Days when you feel discouraged. Days when you wonder if anything has changed.

This doesn't mean you're failing. It means your system is adjusting. Consistency matters more than intensity.

The Real Sign of Progress

The real sign of progress isn't that the past never comes up.
It's that when it does, you don't go with it.

You stay here.
In your body.
In your life.
In your choices.

That's not repression. That's presence.

What This Chapter Asks of You

Not perfection. Not silence. Not control.

Just this:
When your mind goes back, you don't have to follow. That single choice, repeated gently, is how the loop loosens. And once it loosens, something else becomes possible. Not just peace. Presence.

CHAPTER 3

WHAT YOU'RE AFRAID TO LOSE WHEN YOU LET GO

Letting go is rarely resisted because people enjoy holding on.

It's resisted because something important feels at risk.

When people say they're afraid to let go of the past, what they usually mean isn't that they want to keep the pain alive. They mean that the past has become intertwined with things they still rely on: clarity, identity, protection, meaning.

Letting go doesn't feel like relief at first.
It feels like subtraction.

And when you've already lost something significant, the idea of losing *more,* even symbolically, can feel unbearable.

Why Letting Go Can Feel Like Standing on Unstable Ground

For many people, the past functions as an anchor. Not because it's pleasant, but because it's familiar.

It explains:

- Why you're cautious
- Why you don't rush
- Why you notice subtle shifts
- Why you don't trust easily
- Why you hold back parts of yourself

Even pain can feel stabilizing when it provides orientation. So, when someone suggests letting go, your system doesn't hear *freedom.*

It hears:
What will hold me in place if I release this?

That question isn't weakness. It's intelligence shaped by survival.

How Fear Masquerades as Wisdom

One of the reasons this fear is so hard to recognize is that it often presents itself as discernment.

You tell yourself:

- *I've learned to be realistic.*
- *I'm just more careful now.*
- *I know better than I used to.*

And much of that may be true.

But there's a difference between wisdom and vigilance.

Wisdom feels calm and flexible.
Vigilance feels tight and watchful.

When fear drives restraint, letting go feels reckless, even when nothing dangerous is actually happening.

You're Not Holding On to Pain: You're Holding On to What It Gave You

This is the pivot point of the chapter.

People don't cling to suffering. They cling to the *function* suffering served.

Pain may have given you:

- Boundaries you didn't have before
- Awareness you needed at the time
- Permission to say no
- Justification for distance
- A sense of strength or maturity
- Proof that what happened mattered

Letting go can feel like dismantling the very structure that helped you survive.

If pain became the reason you changed, releasing it can feel like undoing your growth. But growth doesn't require ongoing pain to remain valid.

Common Inner Dialogues That Keep the Grip Tight

These fears rarely sound dramatic. They're quiet. Rational. Convincing.

You may recognize thoughts like:

- *If I let this go, I'll be naive again.*
- *If I stop carrying this, I'll lower my standards.*
- *If I soften, I might miss red flags.*
- *This pain taught me something, I can't just drop it.*
- *If I'm not careful, I'll end up back here.*

These thoughts are not irrational. They're attempts to preserve competence. But competence built entirely on fear eventually becomes a cage.

When Pain Becomes Part of Your Identity

Over time, pain doesn't just inform your choices, it shapes how you see yourself.

You may come to identify as:

- Someone who's been through a lot
- Someone who had to grow up early
- Someone who learned the hard way
- Someone who can't afford to be careless

These identities are earned.

But when identity is rooted in injury, moving forward can feel like self-erasure.

You may wonder:
If I'm no longer the person who endured this, who am I?

This isn't a question of weakness, it's a sign that your identity is ready to evolve.

The Loyalty Trap

Another reason letting go feels hard is loyalty.

Loyalty to:

- The version of you who survived
- The pain that shaped you
- The truth of what happened
- The cost you paid

Letting go can feel like betrayal, as if you're abandoning the seriousness of what you endured.

But honoring your past doesn't require carrying it forever. You can respect the chapter without living in it.

How Protection Turns Into Limitation

The past often becomes a reference point for protection.

It answers questions like:

- *Is this safe?*
- *Can I trust this?*
- *Should I stay guarded?*

Initially, this is helpful.

But over time, the same reference point that once protected you begins to limit what you allow.

You may notice:

- You dismiss opportunities before fully considering them
- You keep emotional distance even when connection is available
- You prioritize safety over satisfaction
- You hesitate to want things fully

None of this means you're broken. It means your system is still operating under old conditions.

The Fear Beneath the Fear

If you trace this resistance back far enough, it usually comes down to one concern:

If I let go, I won't know how to protect myself.

This is where the real work begins.

Letting go doesn't mean removing protection.

It means updating it.

The Rules You Made Back Then (And Whether You Still Want Them)

When something hurts you deeply, you don't just feel pain.
You make decisions.

Not always conscious ones, but internal decisions that become rules.

Rules about people. Rules about vulnerability. Rules about what you can expect. Rules about what you must never do again.

These rules often sound like wisdom.
And sometimes they are.

But sometimes they are simply the terms you set in a season when you were trying to survive.

The problem is that survival rules tend to stay in place long after the situation that created them has ended.

Letting go often means revisiting these rules, not to shame yourself for having them, but to decide whether they still deserve authority in your life.

How survival rules form

Survival rules form quickly because the mind is efficient.

If something went badly once, your system tries to prevent the exact conditions from happening again.

It creates "never again" strategies.

You might recognize rules like:

- Don't ask for too much
- Don't rely on people
- Don't get excited too early
- Don't trust words over patterns
- Don't show emotion until you're sure it's safe
- Don't relax until everything is handled

These rules are not random. They are adaptations.

They often saved you from additional disappointment at the time. Rules created in pain tend to be rigid. They protect you and limit you.

Why rules feel safer than choice

Rules reduce uncertainty. Choice requires presence.

When you live by rules, you don't have to assess every moment freshly. You just follow the policy.

But healing invites you back into real-time assessment, and that can feel exposed at first.

If you have been living by protective rules for years, choosing can feel like stepping onto unstable ground.

Because rules feel like control. Choice feels like risk. Even when the current situation is actually safe.

A quick way to identify your rules

You don't need to dig through your whole history to find these. Listen for certain phrases in your mind.

Phrases like:

- "I can't…"
- "I don't do that…"
- "I always…"
- "I never…"
- "People are…"
- "It's not worth…"

These statements often point to a rule. And most rules have a beginning. They were not born with you. They were written by experience.

Rules that protect you vs rules that shrink you

Not every rule needs to be discarded. Some rules are healthy boundaries. The key is whether the rule supports your life or shrinks it.

A protective boundary rule sounds like:
"I don't stay where I am consistently disrespected."

A shrinking survival rule sounds like:
"I don't speak up because it will cause conflict."

Both feel like protection. Only one creates a life you can live in. A boundary expands your dignity. A survival rule often contracts your expression.

The fear underneath changing a rule

Changing a survival rule can trigger a specific fear:
If I stop following this rule, I will return to the old pain.

This fear is understandable.

But it assumes two things that are often no longer true:

- That the world is exactly the same as it was then
- That you're the same person you were then

Part of healing is updating those assumptions.

You may not be able to control outcomes, but you can often trust your response now in a way you couldn't back then.

Rules were necessary when you did not trust your response. Self-trust makes many rules less essential.

A simple rule review

Pick one rule that feels loud in your life right now.

Then ask:

- When did I create this rule?
- Not the exact date, but the season
- "After that relationship"
- "During that job"
- "When I felt powerless"

What was it protecting me from?

Be honest.

- "Being humiliated."
- "Being abandoned."
- "Being blamed."
- "Being trapped."

What is it costing me now?

This is where clarity arrives.

- "It costs me connection."
- "It costs me rest."
- "It costs me honesty."
- "It costs me joy."

What would a present-time version of this rule look like?
Not no rule. Just an updated one.

- Old rule: *"I don't rely on anyone."*

- Updated rule: *"I choose carefully who I rely on, and I ask for what I need."*

This practice isn't about forcing yourself to be open. It's about giving yourself a rule that fits your current reality.

Why loosening rules doesn't make you naive

Many people fear that letting go means forgetting lessons. But you don't lose your learning when you update your rules.

You keep the wisdom. You release the rigidity.
Wisdom is flexible. It adapts to context.
Fear is rigid. It treats all situations like the original injury.

If your system has been treating every close relationship like the one that hurt you, every mistake like the one that cost you, every hope like a setup, loosening rules isn't naivety.

It's accuracy.

Letting yourself want things again

One of the biggest costs of survival rules is that they limit desire. Not just big desire, but ordinary desire.

You stop wanting openly because wanting feels like risk. You stop planning too far ahead because the past taught you that certainty is fragile. You stop letting yourself enjoy what is good because you're braced for it to be taken.

Often, you don't even notice this as deprivation. It feels normal. But a life without desire isn't a protected life. It's a narrowed life.

Letting go includes allowing desire back into the room, gently.

Not with pressure. With permission.

A new kind of safety

Survival rules are designed to prevent pain. But prevention isn't the only kind of safety.

There's also safety that comes from knowing you can recover.

- From knowing you can leave.
- From knowing you can speak up.
- From knowing you can choose yourself without making it a crisis.

This is where letting go becomes less threatening. Not because nothing can go wrong. But because you're no longer depending on rigid rules to keep you okay.

You're depending on your relationship with yourself. And that relationship can be strengthened.

Quietly. One updated rule at a time.

Protection Based on Awareness, Not Fear

There's a difference between: Protection based on fear and Protection based on self-trust.

Fear-based protection says: *I must stay on guard.*

Self-trust-based protection says: *I can respond if something feels wrong.*

The first keeps you vigilant. The second keeps you present. Letting go involves shifting from prevention to response.

What You're Actually Being Asked to Release

Letting go doesn't ask you to release:

- Your discernment
- Your standards
- Your boundaries
- Your insight
- Your self-respect

It asks you to release:

- Hypervigilance
- Constant monitoring
- Emotional bracing
- The belief that pain is required for wisdom

You don't lose intelligence when you let go.
You lose tension.

When Space Feels Uncomfortable

One of the least talked-about parts of letting go is the space it creates. When you stop gripping the past, something opens.

And at first, that space can feel:
- Empty
- Unstructured
- Disorienting

Without constant internal monitoring, you may feel oddly undefined.

This isn't loss. It's availability.

Space is where new preferences emerge, ones not dictated by fear or history.

Why People Rush to Fill the Space

Because space feels unfamiliar, many people rush to fill it.

With busyness.
With new goals.
With self-improvement projects.

But space doesn't need to be filled. It needs to be inhabited.

This is where identity begins to shift, from survival-based to present-based.

Letting Go Without Becoming Careless

A common fear is that letting go will make you careless.
That you'll:

- Miss warning signs
- Lower your standards
- Repeat patterns

But awareness doesn't disappear when pain softens. It becomes more accurate.

Fear blurs perception. Presence sharpens it.

A Grounding Question That Changes the Relationship

Instead of asking:
What if I let go and regret it?

Try asking:
What is this pain still protecting me from?

Then ask:
Is that threat still present, or am I more capable now?

This reframes letting go as reassessment, not risk.

Learning to Carry Yourself Instead

For a long time, the past may have carried you.

It gave structure, meaning, and orientation.

Letting go means choosing to carry yourself now.

Not with force.
Not with certainty.
But with trust.

Trust that you can notice when something feels off.
Trust that you can set boundaries when needed.
Trust that you can leave if you must.

That trust isn't naive.
It's earned.

The Quiet Relief That Follows

When you stop clinging to what once defined you, relief doesn't arrive loudly. It arrives subtly.

You stop rehearsing explanations. You stop bracing in advance. You stop needing your pain to justify your choices.

You feel lighter, not because you forgot, but because you stopped carrying what already taught you enough.

What This Chapter Asks of You

Not to release everything. Not to trust blindly.

Just this: Notice what you're afraid to lose, and question whether it actually depends on pain to exist. Most of the time, it doesn't.

Strength doesn't require suffering. Wisdom doesn't require wounds. Boundaries don't require fear. You're allowed to keep what you gained, without keeping what hurt.

Where This Leaves You

Letting go doesn't mean becoming someone else. It means becoming someone less burdened.

You don't disappear. You emerge, without the weight that once helped you survive but no longer needs to come with you. And that shift, quiet, gradual, and deeply personal, is how the grip finally loosens.

CHAPTER 4

CLOSURE ISN'T A CONVERSATION YOU FINISH

For many people, letting go feels impossible because something still feels unfinished.

Not emotionally unresolved in a dramatic sense, but incomplete. As if there's a final conversation that never happened, a moment of understanding that never arrived, or an explanation that would finally make everything settle.

You may believe that if you could just say the right thing, or hear the right thing, you'd be able to move on.

This belief is deeply human. It's also one of the most persistent traps that keeps the past active.

Why Closure Gets Misunderstood

Closure is often imagined as a moment.

A conversation.
An apology.
An admission.
A realization.

Something definitive that draws a line between then and now.

But in reality, closure is rarely something another person gives you. It's something your system allows. And that permission doesn't come from answers, it comes from acceptance of *what is no longer available*.

The Loop of Waiting

When closure is externalized, the past stays open. You may find yourself waiting for:

- Someone to understand what they did
- Someone to acknowledge your pain
- Someone to explain themselves clearly
- Someone to take responsibility
- Someone to change

As long as closure depends on someone else's behavior, your nervous system remains in a holding pattern.

Not because you're powerless, but because you're oriented toward an outcome you can't control. Waiting isn't neutral. It quietly prolongs the grip.

Why Imagined Conversations Keep Happening

Many people replay conversations that never occurred. They imagine:

- What they would say now
- How the other person might respond
- What they wish had been understood

These internal dialogues can feel productive, even empowering. But most of the time, they're attempts to finish something that didn't end cleanly.

The mind returns because it believes resolution is still possible.

Letting go doesn't mean you stop wanting understanding. It means you stop organizing your emotional life around its absence.

When Answers Don't Actually Bring Relief

Here's something that surprises many people:
Even when answers are given, relief is often temporary.

An apology comes - but it doesn't land.
An explanation is offered - but it doesn't soothe.
A truth is revealed - but it doesn't free you.

Why?

Because the need for closure was never about information. It was about safety. Answers don't always restore safety, especially when trust has already been disrupted.

The Unfinished Feeling Isn't a Sign You Need More

The sense of something being unfinished is often interpreted as a signal to keep engaging. But more often, it's a sign that engagement itself is what's keeping the wound open.

Some experiences don't end with clarity.
They end with *limits*.

Limits on what you'll understand.
Limits on what you'll receive.
Limits on what can be repaired.

Acknowledging those limits is painful, but it's also stabilizing.

The Difference Between Understanding and Completion

You can fully understand what happened and still feel affected by it.

Completion isn't about comprehension.
It's about disengagement.

You don't need to fully understand someone else's behavior to stop letting it define your emotional landscape.

Understanding answers *why*.

Completion answers *whether you're still participating*.

Why Closure Can Feel Like Justice

For many people, closure isn't just emotional, it's moral.

It feels tied to:

- Fairness
- Validation
- Being seen
- Being believed

Without closure, it can feel like the story ended incorrectly. Like something true was left unacknowledged.

This is where letting go can feel deeply unjust. But justice doesn't require proximity.

You don't have to stay emotionally engaged with someone to know the truth of what you experienced.

The Hidden Cost of Staying Open

Remaining open to closure has consequences.
You may notice:

- Difficulty fully committing to the present
- Emotional availability being split
- A sense of waiting without knowing what for
- Revisiting the same emotional terrain repeatedly

The past remains active not because it's unresolved, but because it's still being referenced. Letting go begins when you stop checking whether something has changed.

Closure as an Internal Decision

Real closure begins with a quiet internal shift:

I am no longer waiting for this to resolve differently.

This doesn't mean you approve of what happened.

It means you accept that the ending already occurred, even if you didn't like it.

That acceptance doesn't come all at once. It comes in layers.

When Letting Go Feels Like Giving Up

One of the hardest parts of this chapter is naming the fear underneath resistance to closure:

If I stop waiting, it means I'm accepting that this is how it ended.

That can feel like defeat.

But acceptance isn't agreement.

It's realism. And realism creates stability.

What You're Actually Releasing

Letting go of the need for closure doesn't mean releasing:

- Your truth
- Your memory
- Your perspective
- Your standards

It means releasing:

- The hope that someone else will fix the ending
- The expectation that the past will resolve retroactively
- The belief that emotional relief requires someone else's participation

You don't lose truth when you stop waiting.
You gain your present back.

When You Stop Revisiting the Scene

Closure begins to take hold when you notice a subtle shift.

You stop replaying.
You stop rehearsing.
You stop imagining alternative endings.

Not because you force yourself to, but because you no longer expect anything new to emerge.

The scene becomes complete, not satisfying, but finished.

Grieving the Ending You Didn't Get

This is important.

Letting go often requires grieving, not what happened, but what *didn't*.

The conversation you didn't have.
The accountability that never came.
The repair that wasn't possible.

Grief acknowledges that loss without keeping you tethered to it.

You don't grieve to stay connected.
You grieve to release.

The Grief That Doesn't Get Recognized

Some grief gets sympathy immediately.
Other grief gets questioned.

It gets minimized because it doesn't look like what people expect grief to look like.

You might be grieving someone who is still alive. Grieving a relationship you ended on purpose. Grieving a version of family that never existed. Grieving years you can't get back. Grieving the person you were before you learned to be careful.

This kind of grief can feel disorienting because it doesn't come with clear permission.

If you didn't "choose" the loss in a clean way, you might feel conflicted about whether you're allowed to grieve it at all.

But grief isn't a verdict on whether something was good for you. Grief is a response to attachment. And attachment isn't always logical.

Ambiguous grief

There's a type of grief that comes from uncertainty and lack of clarity.

It shows up when you lost something without a clear ending.

When there was no goodbye that made sense. No closure that felt complete. No clean shift from "we are connected" to "we are not."

You might still feel emotionally connected to someone you don't want back in your life. You might miss a person and also feel relieved they are gone. You might mourn the potential while feeling clear about the reality.

This isn't confusion. It's complexity. And complexity is often what makes grief linger.

Grieving what you hoped it would become

Sometimes what you're grieving isn't what happened. It's what you hoped would happen.

You hoped they would grow. You hoped the effort would be met. You hoped the love would be enough. You hoped the hard season would pass and something stable would remain.

When those hopes collapse, the loss isn't just relational. It's existential.

You're grieving:

- The future you pictured
- The version of yourself who would have been safer there
- The story you expected your life to follow
- This grief can feel childish or embarrassing

It's not.

Hope is a form of investment. When you invested heavily, the loss is real even if the outcome was inevitable.

Secondary grief

Secondary grief is grief for what the primary loss triggered.

For example:
- You lost a relationship, and then you lost a social circle
- You lost a job, and then you lost your sense of confidence
- You lost trust, and then you lost your ability to relax
- You lost safety, and then you lost parts of your personality

Secondary grief is why people sometimes feel like they are grieving "too much" for the original event.

They are not grieving one thing.
They are grieving the chain of consequences.

This is also why you can grieve long after life looks stable again. The original event is over, but you're still living with what it rearranged.

The grief of not being chosen

Some of the deepest grief isn't about what you lost. It's about what you were not given.

Not being chosen. Not being protected. Not being valued. Not being understood.

These are not small losses. They can shape how you move through life. And they can be difficult to grieve because there's no object to point to. No single moment to mourn.

It's a slow grief.
A grief that accumulates.

If you were taught to minimize your needs, you might not even label this as grief. You might call it insecurity, or sensitivity, or being "too much."

But grief is often the honest name.

Why grief can show up after you let go

Many people expect grief to come first, and relief to come later. In reality, relief often comes first.

You step away. You detach. You stop engaging. You feel lighter. Then grief arrives. This can be confusing. You may wonder if you made the wrong decision.

But grief arriving after you let go is common because your system finally has enough safety to feel what it couldn't feel while you were still in it.

When you were surviving, grief was too costly. Now, it becomes possible. Grief isn't always a sign that you should go back. Often it's a sign that you're finally free enough to process.

What grief is trying to do

Grief isn't just sadness.
Grief is integration.

It's your system trying to accept what can't be changed. It's your system trying to update the story of your life so the loss has a place, rather than floating around as unfinished business.

When grief is resisted, it tends to stretch out.
When grief is allowed, it tends to move.

Not quickly. Not neatly. But it moves.

A grounded way to meet grief without drowning in it

If you have avoided grief because you fear it will pull you under, you don't need to leap into it. You can meet it in contained ways.

Try this:
- Set a timer for ten minutes
- Ask, *"What am I grieving that I haven't named?"*
- Write a few sentences. Not pages
- Stop when the timer ends, even if you could continue
- Do something physical after, like washing dishes or taking a walk

This isn't avoidance. It's pacing. Pacing teaches your system that grief is tolerable. That it has edges. That it doesn't have to become your whole day.

What you're allowed to grieve

You're allowed to grieve:
- Someone who hurt you
- A life you did not get to have
- A version of yourself you had to abandon
- The years you spent braced
- The effort that did not lead to repair
- The innocence you lost
- The time it took to accept reality

None of this means you want the past back. It means you're honoring the cost. And honoring the cost is often what allows you to stop paying it.

When grief becomes gentler

Grief doesn't disappear through force. It softens through recognition.

Eventually, the grief becomes less about searching and more about remembering.

Less sharp. Less urgent. Less tied to what might have been.

You don't need to rush this. Grief has its own pace.

But you can support it by giving it permission. Not endless attention. Just honest acknowledgment. That's often the missing ingredient that keeps attachment alive.

Once grief is allowed, attachment no longer has to fight to be seen. And the past can finally settle where it belongs.

In your history, not in your nervous system.

Closure Without Contact

Many people believe closure requires contact.
It doesn't.

Closure can occur:

- *Without* explanation
- *Without* apology
- *Without* reconciliation
- *Without* acknowledgment

What it requires is an internal decision to stop orienting toward the past.

You decide, not emotionally, but structurally, that this chapter no longer gets to shape your present.

A Question That Changes the Orientation

Instead of asking:
What do I still need from them?

Try asking:
What am I still giving my energy to?

This shifts closure from something you're missing to something you're offering.

And you're allowed to stop offering it.

When Peace Feels Like Letting Someone "Get Away With It"

Another common resistance is the belief that letting go lets someone off the hook.

But peace isn't exoneration.

You can hold someone accountable *internally* without continuing to suffer. Your well-being isn't a reward you owe anyone.

What Completion Actually Feels Like

Completion doesn't feel triumphant. It feels neutral.

The memory still exists, but it no longer demands engagement.

You don't brace when it comes up.
You don't feel pulled to revisit it.
You don't need it to make sense anymore.

It becomes something that happened, not something that's happening.

What This Chapter Asks of You

Not to forgive prematurely.
Not to approve of the ending.
Not to force acceptance.

Only this: Notice where you're still waiting, and consider whether waiting is serving you.

Closure doesn't arrive when someone else changes.
It arrives when you stop expecting them to.

Where This Leaves You

You don't need to finish a conversation that already ended. You don't need answers that never came.

You're allowed to close a chapter even if it ended poorly. And when you do, you don't lose truth. You reclaim your present.

CHAPTER 5

FORGIVENESS ISN'T WHAT YOU THINK IT IS

For many people, forgiveness is where letting go gets stuck.

Not because they don't understand the concept, but because the way forgiveness is commonly described feels wrong, premature, or even dangerous.

You may have been told that forgiveness is necessary for healing. That it's the final step. That without it, you'll remain bitter, trapped, or incomplete.

And yet, when you imagine forgiving what happened, something inside you resists.

That resistance isn't immaturity. It's discernment.

Why Forgiveness Feels Like a Threat

Forgiveness is often framed as something you *owe*. An obligation to be kind. A moral requirement. A sign that you've grown.

But when forgiveness is framed this way, it can feel like erasure. As if forgiving means:

- Minimizing what happened
- Excusing harmful behavior
- Pretending you weren't affected
- Releasing accountability
- Invalidating your own pain

If forgiveness requires self-betrayal, of course you resist it. That resistance is protective.

The Cultural Confusion Around Forgiveness

One of the reasons forgiveness feels so complicated is that it's been flattened into a single idea.

People use the word *forgiveness* to mean many different things:

- Reconciliation
- Forgetting
- Releasing anger
- Restoring trust
- Offering grace
- Spiritual virtue

But these are not the same.

And confusing them places enormous pressure on people who are still healing. Letting go doesn't require adopting someone else's definition of forgiveness.

Forgiveness Isn't Reconciliation

This distinction is critical. Forgiveness doesn't require:

- Contact
- Relationship
- Access
- Trust
- Repair

You can forgive and still choose distance.
You can forgive and still say no.
You can forgive and never speak to someone again.

Reconciliation requires two willing participants.
Forgiveness doesn't.

Forgiveness Isn't Forgetting

Forgetting is passive and unreliable. Forgiveness isn't about deleting memory.

You don't forget what taught you how to protect yourself. You don't forget what shaped your boundaries.

Memory isn't the problem. Re-engagement is.

Forgiveness Isn't Approval

This is where many people draw a hard line, and understandably so.

Forgiving doesn't mean:

- What happened was okay
- You deserved it
- It wasn't harmful
- It shouldn't have affected you

Forgiveness doesn't rewrite reality.
It changes your relationship to it.

Why Pressure to Forgive Delays Healing

When forgiveness is framed as mandatory, people often rush toward it prematurely.

They say they forgive, but their body hasn't caught up.
This creates internal conflict.

One part of you tries to move on. Another part still feels unheard.

This isn't healing. It's compliance.

True letting go cannot be forced, especially not by moral pressure.

What Forgiveness Actually Addresses

Forgiveness isn't about the other person.
It's about your *continued involvement.*

Specifically:

- How much emotional energy the past still receives
- How often you revisit the injury
- How much resentment you're required to carry

Forgiveness doesn't remove accountability.
It removes occupation.

The Difference Between Anger and Attachment

Anger often gets framed as the opposite of forgiveness.
But the real opposite of forgiveness isn't anger.

It's attachment.

You can feel anger briefly and let it pass.

But attachment keeps you tethered.

Forgiveness begins when you stop needing the past to validate your emotions.

When Anger Is Still Doing Important Work

Sometimes anger is necessary.

It protects boundaries.
It signals violation.
It restores self-respect.

Forgiveness that bypasses anger doesn't resolve it, it buries it.

Letting go doesn't require abandoning anger before it's finished doing its job.

It requires noticing when anger has turned into obligation.

Forgiveness as Release, Not Gift

Forgiveness is often described as a gift you give someone else.

This framing is misleading.

Forgiveness is a release you give yourself.

A release from:

- Replaying the injury
- Carrying resentment daily
- Organizing your emotional life around what happened

The other person doesn't need to receive anything for forgiveness to occur.

A Private Closure Ritual That Doesn't Require Contact

If closure has been externalized for a long time, the idea of internal closure can sound hollow. It can feel like pretending. Like settling. Like telling yourself a story you don't fully believe.

So, it helps to approach closure differently. Not as a mindset, but as a structure.

Because your system often needs structure to recognize an ending. This is where a private closure ritual can be useful. Not a dramatic ceremony.

A quiet, deliberate act that signals, this chapter is complete enough for me to stop engaging with it.

Why rituals work when insight doesn't

Rituals work because they create a boundary in time. They mark transition. They tell the mind and body, something has shifted.

When an ending is unclear, a ritual creates a clear line you did not get the first time. This is especially helpful when:

- The ending was slow
- The ending was confusing
- The ending was one-sided
- The ending involved silence
- The ending was never acknowledged

A ritual doesn't change reality. It changes your relationship to the reality you already have.

STEP ONE: The Reality Inventory

Write down what is true, without argument.
Keep it simple. Short statements.

Examples:
- They did not take responsibility.
- I did not get the conversation I wanted.
- The pattern did not change.
- I waited longer than I needed to.
- I did what I could with what I knew.

This isn't a list of accusations. It's a list of facts you keep trying to negotiate with.

Closure begins when reality is allowed to be real.

STEP TWO: The Unsent Ending

Write an ending statement that you will never send. Not because you're afraid. Because closure isn't dependent on their response.

This statement isn't a full letter unless you want it to be. It can be a paragraph.

It should include three elements:

- What you acknowledge
  - This mattered.
  - This changed me.
  - This cost me.

- What you're no longer waiting for
  - I'm no longer waiting for understanding.
  - I'm no longer waiting for accountability.
  - I'm no longer waiting for the ending to improve.

- What you're choosing now
  - I'm choosing distance.
  - I'm choosing my present.
  - I'm choosing to stop revisiting this.

The power here isn't in perfect wording.
It's in finality.

STEP THREE: The Energy Return

Closure isn't just about the story. It's about where your energy goes.

So, choose one sentence that returns your energy to you.

Examples:

- I release the role of convincing.
- I release the role of waiting.
- I release the role of reliving.
- I take my attention back.

Say it quietly, out loud if you can.

The body often registers spoken finality differently than internal thought.

STEP FOUR: A practical boundary

If closure has been kept open through access, create one boundary that reduces re-entry.

This might be:

- Deleting a thread you keep rereading
- Removing a bookmark you keep checking
- Muting an account that keeps you hooked
- Putting reminders in a folder you don't scroll through
- Choosing not to ask mutual friends for updates

This isn't about being strong. It's about making it easier for your system to disengage.

If the past is always available, your mind will keep reopening it.

STEP FIVE: A replacement action

Do one small thing right after the ritual that anchors you in your present.

Nothing performative. Nothing huge. Something physical, ordinary, and real. Make dinner. Take a shower. Go for a walk. Clean a drawer. The point is to signal: we are back in our life now.

This matters because closure isn't just emotional.
It's directional.

What if you still feel unfinished afterward?

You might. This ritual isn't a magic switch. But it creates a new posture.

Instead of waiting, you're choosing. Instead of hoping for a different ending, you're creating a clear one internally.

If unfinished feelings remain, treat them as grief, not as a signal to re-engage. Unfinished doesn't always mean unresolved.

Sometimes it means you're still adjusting to the boundary you just set.

Closure as self-respect

One of the most overlooked truths is that closure is often an act of self-respect.

It's you saying:

- *I will not keep paying attention to something that cannot meet me.*
- *I will not keep reopening my own wound to see if it hurts less today.*
- *I will not keep giving my present away to something that already took enough.*

Closure isn't a conversation you finish. Sometimes it's simply the moment you stop returning.

Not with bitterness. With dignity. And with a quiet willingness to let your life be bigger than the ending you did not get.

When Forgiveness Happens Naturally

True forgiveness rarely arrives as a decision.
It arrives as a shift.

You notice:

- The story has less charge
- The memory doesn't hook you
- The anger doesn't need fueling
- The past doesn't demand commentary

This isn't something you force. It's something that happens when the grip loosens.

Why Some Things Don't Need Forgiveness at All

Here's a truth that often brings relief:
Not everything needs to be forgiven.

Some things simply need to be *released*. Release doesn't require moral framing. It doesn't require generosity. It doesn't require grace. It requires distance.

You're allowed to say:

- *This no longer belongs in my life.*
- *I don't need to forgive this to move on.*

Letting go isn't dependent on forgiveness.
Forgiveness is optional.

When Forgiveness Is Actually Self-Forgiveness

Sometimes the hardest forgiveness isn't toward someone else, but toward yourself.

You may still carry:

- Regret for staying
- Shame for not seeing things sooner
- Anger at yourself for choices you made with limited information

Letting go often requires releasing the expectation that you should have known better.

You did what you could with what you had.
That matters.

Releasing the Need to Be "The Bigger Person"

Forgiveness is often tied to maturity.

Being told to forgive can feel like being told to rise above what hurt you.

But healing isn't about moral hierarchy.

You don't need to be bigger than what happened.

You need to be **free from it.**

A Question That Clarifies Readiness

Instead of asking:
Should I forgive?

Try asking:
Is holding onto this still serving me?

This removes obligation and restores agency.
You don't forgive because you should.
You release because you're ready.

What Letting Go Looks Like Without Forgiveness

Letting go may look like:

- Indifference rather than compassion
- Distance rather than closure
- Acceptance rather than grace

These aren't failures. They are forms of completion.

When Forgiveness Becomes Unnecessary

At a certain point, the question of forgiveness simply stops mattering.

Not because the past disappeared, but because it lost relevance.

You're no longer orienting toward it. You're living from here.

What This Chapter Asks of You

Not to forgive prematurely.
Not to force compassion.
Not to absolve anyone.

Only this:

Release the belief that forgiveness is required for freedom.
You don't need to make peace with the past.
You need to stop letting it occupy your present.

Where This Leaves You

Forgiveness isn't a finish line.
It's a byproduct, sometimes.

And sometimes, it's not needed at all.

- You're allowed to let go without forgiving.

- You're allowed to move forward without rewriting history.

- And you're allowed to choose peace without moral negotiation.

CHAPTER 6

LEARNING TO LIVE WITHOUT REOPENING OLD WOUNDS

One of the quiet fears people rarely admit, especially after they've done a lot of emotional work, isn't about the past itself. It's about its return.

Even after you've loosened the grip, stopped replaying old stories, and reclaimed space in your life, there's often a lingering concern that sits just beneath the surface:

- *What if this comes back?*
- *What if a memory resurfaces unexpectedly?*
- *What if something familiar triggers the old response?*
- *What if one careless moment pulls you right back into a version of yourself you thought you'd left behind?*

This fear doesn't mean you doubt your progress. It means you don't yet trust its durability.

And that makes sense.

Why We Mistake Triggers for Regression

Many people believe healing means reaching a point where the past no longer touches them at all.

So, when an old reaction appears, tightness in the chest, a sudden emotional spike, a familiar thought pattern, they assume something has gone wrong.

They think:

- *I thought I was past this*
- *Why is this still here?*
- *Did I undo my progress?*

But this interpretation misunderstands how healing actually works.

Triggers are not evidence that healing failed.

They are evidence that your system learned deeply, and is now learning *differently*.

What a Trigger Actually Is

A trigger isn't the past returning. It's the body checking for safety.

Something in your present moment resembles a past experience, not logically, but sensorially. A tone of voice. A facial expression. A silence. A familiar dynamic.

Your system reacts before your conscious mind has time to evaluate. That reaction doesn't mean danger is present. It means your body is asking a question.

Healing Isn't the Absence of Triggers: It's the Presence of Choice

This distinction is everything.

Before healing, a trigger meant:

- Emotional flooding
- Loss of presence
- Automatic reaction
- Over analysis or shutdown

After healing begins, a trigger becomes something else.
It becomes:

- A sensation you notice
- A moment you pause in
- A choice point

The trigger still happens. What changes is what happens *next*.

How Triggers Show Up in Everyday Life

Triggers are rarely dramatic. They often appear as:

- Feeling suddenly small in a neutral conversation
- Overreacting internally to mild criticism
- Wanting to explain yourself when no one asked
- Feeling defensive without knowing why
- Going quiet when you meant to speak

These moments don't mean you're back where you started. They mean your system is testing whether old patterns are still required.

The Trap of Self-Judgment

One of the fastest ways to reopen an old wound is judging yourself for feeling it.

When you think:

- *I shouldn't feel this anymore.*
- *This means I haven't healed.*
- *I'm failing at letting go.*

You add a second layer of distress on top of the first.

Instead of asking *What's wrong with me?*, try asking: *What does my body think is happening right now?*

That single shift moves you from shame to understanding.

Staying Present Without Reopening the Story

When a trigger hits, the instinct is to explain it. To analyze the past. To make sense of why this is happening *again*.

But explanation often reopens the very door you worked to close. Instead of interpretation, focus on orientation.

You might quietly tell yourself:
- *I'm safe right now.*
- *This is old information.*
- *I don't need to go back there.*

You're not suppressing anything.
You're anchoring yourself in the present.

Why Old Feelings Surface During Good Times

One of the most confusing experiences is when old emotions appear *after* life has stabilized.

You may feel:
- Sad during calm
- Anxious when things are going well
- Guarded when safety is finally present

This isn't regression. It's release.

When your system is no longer preoccupied with survival, it finally has space to process what it couldn't before.

Old material surfaces not because something is wrong, but because something is *right*.

Learning to Trust Calm Again

For people who lived in heightened states for a long time, calm can feel suspicious.

Quiet feels unfamiliar.
Neutral feels unsafe.
Peace feels temporary.

Your system learned that vigilance was necessary. Letting go of that stance takes time. Calm isn't a warning sign. It's a signal that nothing is required of you in this moment.

Avoidance vs. Stability

Early in healing, avoidance can be protective. But long-term avoidance shrinks your life.

You don't need to avoid reminders forever. You need to encounter them without being pulled under.

Stability isn't about never being reminded. It's about staying present when you are.

Three Separate Lanes: Release, Accountability, and Repair

One reason forgiveness becomes so loaded is that it's often asked to do three jobs at once.

- To release your resentment.
- To absolve the other person.
- To restore the relationship.

But these are three different processes. When they get blended, you end up stuck.

Because part of you wants relief, part of you wants accountability, and part of you is unsure whether repair was ever possible.

So, it helps to separate them into lanes. Not to make forgiveness more complicated, but to make it clearer.

LANE ONE: Release

Release is what you do for your own nervous system. It's the gradual decision to stop feeding the injury with daily attention.

Release can include:

- *No longer* replaying the same moments
- *No longer* rehearsing what you would say
- *No longer* checking whether they changed
- *No longer* needing the past to validate your boundaries

Release isn't generosity. Release is unclenching.

It's allowing your body to stop living as if the injury is still active.

You can release without soft feelings. You can release while still believing what they did was wrong.

Release is about your involvement, not their character.

LANE TWO: Accountability

Accountability is about truth. It's about naming what happened without minimizing it.

This lane matters because people often fear that releasing resentment means erasing the seriousness of what occurred.

It doesn't. You can hold accountability internally.

You can say:

- *"That was not okay."*
- *"They crossed a line."*
- *"That behavior had consequences."*
- *"I deserved better."*

Accountability doesn't require confrontation.
It requires clarity.

This lane also includes boundaries. Not boundaries as punishment, but boundaries as reality.

If someone showed you who they are, accountability means you live as if you believe it.

LANE THREE: Repair

Repair is what happens when two people rebuild something.

This lane requires:

- Consistent change
- Emotional honesty
- Mutual effort
- A willingness to be impacted
- Time

Repair isn't owed to anyone. And it's not always possible.

Some people cannot repair because they won't acknowledge harm. Some cannot repair because their version of events requires your silence. Some cannot repair because the dynamic was the point.

If repair isn't available, that doesn't mean you must stay in Lane one forever, waiting for Lane three.

You can release without repair.
This is often the missing permission.

Why this separation calms the internal conflict

If you have been resisting forgiveness, it may be because forgiveness felt like a demand to merge the lanes.

To release, and absolve, and reconnect. When you separate the lanes, you can choose what is true for you. You might decide:

- *I want release, but I don't want repair.*
- *I want accountability, but I don't want contact.*
- *I want distance, and that is enough.*

This isn't bitterness. It's precision.

How to work with the lanes in a grounded way

Try these questions, one lane at a time.

For release: *"What am I still doing that keeps this active?"*

You're not looking for shame.
You're looking for a lever.
Even one small lever matters.

For accountability: *"What do I need to stop pretending was acceptable?"*

Accountability is often less about the other person and more about you telling the truth to yourself.

Especially if you spent years rationalizing, excusing, or enduring.

For repair:
"Is repair available, and if so, what evidence supports that?"

Not hope. Evidence.

If the evidence isn't there, you don't have to keep your life in a holding pattern.

A relief that many people don't expect

When you stop forcing forgiveness to do all three jobs, you may feel something shift.

You realize you can have peace without pretending. You can have calm without reopening doors. You can release the daily emotional labor without excusing the harm.

That is what maturity actually looks like. Not being endlessly understanding. Being clear.

What if you feel guilty for not repairing?

Some people carry guilt for choosing distance, especially if they were trained to prioritize harmony over self-respect.

But repair isn't a requirement for being a good person. Repair is an option, and it requires conditions.

If the conditions are not present, choosing distance isn't cruelty. It's self-protection without drama.

Forgiveness as a possible byproduct

Once the lanes are separated, forgiveness becomes less central. Sometimes it happens naturally as release deepens. Sometimes it doesn't.

Either way, you aren't stuck. You're simply living in the lane that supports your life.

If you take one thing from this section, let it be this:

- You can release without reconciling.
- You can hold truth without staying tethered.
- You can move forward without rewriting what happened.

That isn't moral failure. That's freedom with boundaries.

When the Past Tries to Re-Negotiate

Sometimes the past returns not as pain, but as nostalgia.

You might think:

- *It wasn't all bad*
- *I miss who I was then*
- *Maybe I overreacted*

These thoughts aren't invitations. They're negotiations.

The past is checking whether it still has influence.

You don't need to argue. You simply don't follow.

Building a Present That Feels Safe to Live In

One of the most powerful stabilization tools isn't internal work, it's environmental support.

A present that feels predictable, honest, and liveable gives your system something solid to land in.

This might look like:
- Clear routines
- Relationships with emotional consistency
- Boundaries you don't have to defend
- Rest without justification
- Pleasure without explanation

The more your present supports you, the less the past intrudes.

From Prevention to Recovery

Before healing, your energy went into prevention.

Preventing mistakes.
Preventing pain.
Preventing disappointment.

After healing, the work shifts to recovery. You trust that:

- You can feel discomfort and stay present
- You can notice red flags without panic
- You can respond if something goes wrong

Recovery builds confidence faster than avoidance ever could.

Redefining Strength

Strength is not never being affected. Strength is noticing sooner, responding more gently, and returning to yourself faster.

You don't fail because you feel something old. You succeed because you don't let it run your life.

What Progress Actually Looks Like

Progress doesn't mean triggers disappear. It means:

- They pass more quickly
- They feel less convincing
- They don't hijack your behavior
- They don't rewrite your identity

You stay oriented to who you are *now*.

When You Do Get Pulled Back

There will be moments when you do get pulled back. That doesn't erase your progress. Healing isn't a straight line. It's a widening range of responses.

When this happens:

- Be kind instead of corrective
- Ground instead of analyze
- Return instead of review

The faster you return, the less power the past holds.

A Gentle End-of-Day Check-In

At the end of the day, try asking yourself:
Did I reopen anything today, or did I stay present?

This isn't a judgment.

It's awareness. And awareness is what sustains healing.

When Living Forward Becomes Natural

Eventually, something shifts.

You stop tracking your healing.
You stop watching for triggers.
You stop asking whether you're *"over it."*

You're just living.
The past still exists, but it no longer interrupts.

What This Chapter Asks of You

Not to eliminate triggers. Not to control your reactions.

Only this:
When something old appears, you don't have to go with it.

You stay here.
In your body.
In your life.
In your choices.

That steadiness, that ability to remain present even when echoes appear, isn't fragile.

It's learned.
And once learned, it stays.

Where This Leaves You

Letting go doesn't mean the past never shows up.

It means when it does, it doesn't take you with it.

And that is how healing becomes liveable, not perfect, but real.

CHAPTER 7

BECOMING SOMEONE WHO ISN'T DEFINED BY WHAT HURT THEM

There's a moment in the letting-go process that feels strangely anticlimactic.

Nothing dramatic happens. There's no emotional breakthrough, no clear sense of arrival, no sudden feeling of triumph. Life doesn't change in a way you can point to. Instead, something quieter occurs.

A memory comes up, and you don't follow it. A familiar situation arises, and you don't brace the way you used to. An old story appears, and it doesn't ask to be explained.

You don't feel victorious. You feel steady. And that steadiness can be surprisingly disorienting.

When the Past Stops Leading, Something Else Has to

For a long time, the past may have acted as an internal compass. It told you:

- What to avoid
- What to be careful with
- What not to expect
- How much to reveal
- What kind of person you needed to be

Even when it was heavy, it gave you orientation.

So, when the past loosens its grip, when it stops being consulted automatically, there's often a gap.

And in that gap, a question quietly emerges:
If I'm no longer defined by what hurt me... who am I now?

This question doesn't mean you're lost. It means you're no longer being directed by survival.

Identity After Survival Feels Unfamiliar, Not Empty

One of the biggest misconceptions about healing is that it replaces pain with clarity.

In reality, healing often replaces pain with space.

And space can feel unsettling when you've spent years organized around adaptation.

You may notice:

- You're less reactive, but also less certain
- Your old explanations don't fit as well
- You don't know how much of your story to share
- You feel calmer, but less defined

This isn't emptiness. It's reorganization.

Your identity is adjusting to a life that no longer requires constant defense.

When Survival Became an Identity

For many people, survival wasn't just something they did.

It became who they were.

You may have unconsciously identified as:

- The strong one
- The careful one
- The one who endured
- The one who learned the hard way
- The one who couldn't afford to be naive

These identities weren't imagined. They were earned.

But survival identities aren't meant to be permanent.

They are roles you play when something is required of you, not the essence of who you are.

Why Letting Go Can Feel Like Losing Yourself

This is why identity-level fear often emerges *late* in the healing process. When the pain softens, you're no longer fighting.

And when you're no longer fighting, the version of you that existed *because* of the fight has less to do.

This can feel like loss. Not of pain, but of familiarity.

You may wonder:

- *If I'm not the person who survived this, who am I?*
- *What defines me now?*
- *What anchors me if not my story?*

These questions are not signs something is wrong. They're signs something new is forming.

Remembering Without Referencing

One of the clearest markers of integration is the shift from referencing the past to simply remembering it.

Remembering is neutral.
Referencing is directive.

When you reference the past, it guides decisions. When you remember it, it informs, but doesn't instruct.

Integration doesn't require forgetting. It requires repositioning. The past moves from authority to context.

When You Stop Leading With Your Story

As the past becomes less central, you may notice you share it differently.

You no longer lead with what happened.
You don't automatically explain yourself through it.
You don't offer your pain as context for your choices.

This can feel awkward at first.

You may be used to your story doing work for you, explaining, justifying, protecting. Without it, interactions can feel strangely unstructured.

But this isn't absence. It's autonomy.

Identity Built From Preference, Not Protection

One of the quiet shifts in this stage is how decisions get made. Before, choices were often guided by protection:

- *Is this safe?*
- *Will this hurt me?*
- *What's the risk?*

Now, a different question begins to surface: *What do I actually want?* Preference is quieter than protection.

It doesn't shout.
It doesn't rush.
It doesn't demand certainty.

It simply feels right without explanation.

Learning to trust preference is a sign that you're no longer living in reaction.

When Peace Feels Suspicious

For people who lived in heightened states for a long time, peace can feel strange.

You may notice yourself scanning for what's wrong. Waiting for interruption. Feeling uneasy when nothing is required of you.

This isn't intuition. It's conditioning.

Your system learned that calm was temporary, and vigilance was necessary. Letting yourself trust neutrality takes time. Peace doesn't mean something is missing. It means nothing is demanding you.

A Plan for the Moment You Get Hit

It's one thing to understand triggers intellectually. It's another thing to be in the moment when your body reacts before you do.

A tone changes, and your chest tightens. A silence stretches and your mind starts sprinting. Someone disappoints you in a small way, and suddenly you feel the old urgency rise.

In those moments, it helps to have a plan. Not a complex plan. A simple sequence that keeps you from reopening the story.

Think of it as a response you practice, so you don't have to invent one while activated.

STEP ONE: Pause the storyline

When you get hit, your mind will want to explain. It will want to connect the present moment to the past.

It will start narrating:

"This is just like before."
"I knew this would happen."
"Here we go again."

That narration isn't truth. It's pattern recognition under stress. So, your first job is to pause the storyline.

Try a single sentence:
"This is a reaction. Not a conclusion."

That sentence creates space.

STEP TWO: Locate the reaction in your body

Your body is often ahead of your thoughts.

So, bring attention to sensation. Where do you feel it?

- Throat tight
- Jaw clenched
- Chest heavy
- Stomach dropped
- Hands restless

This isn't about analyzing why.

It's about grounding in what's actually happening right now. Naming sensation reduces the feeling of being swallowed by it.

STEP THREE: Orient to present reality

Triggers are often time confusion. Your system thinks it's back there. So orient.

Look around and name:

- Where you are?
- What year is it?
- What's the actual situation?

You might quietly say:

"I'm in my kitchen."
"It's this year."
"This is a conversation, not a crisis."

Again, this isn't positive thinking.
It's time correction.

STEP FOUR: Choose one regulating action

Regulation isn't about becoming calm immediately. It's about giving your system a signal that you're handling the moment.

Choose one action:

- Slow your exhale for three breaths
- Put both feet on the ground and press down
- Take a sip of water
- Step outside for sixty seconds
- Place a hand on your chest and feel the contact

Small actions matter because they're real. They interrupt the momentum.

STEP FIVE: Decide what the moment needs

Once you have a little space, ask:
"What does this moment require?"

Not what the past requires. This moment. It might require:

- A boundary
- A pause
- A clarifying question
- Time alone
- A direct statement
- Nothing at all

Sometimes the most self-respecting move is doing less, not more. Not defending. Not explaining. Not fixing. Just pausing.

What if you still feel pulled?

You might.

The point isn't to eliminate the pull. The point is to reduce the chance that you follow it all the way back.

If you do get pulled into old thoughts, you can return with the same sequence again.

Return is a skill. You build it through repetition.

A script for when you need space

If you tend to override yourself and stay in situations that activate you, it helps to have a simple script ready.

Here are a few options you can adapt:

- *"I need a minute. I'll come back to this."*

- *"I'm noticing I'm getting flooded. I want to respond well, so I'm going to pause."*

- *"I can't talk about this clearly right now. Let's pick it up later."*

This isn't dramatic. It's self-leadership.

How this prevents reopening old wounds

Old wounds reopen when you do one of two things: You re-enter the story and relive it, or you act from activation and then punish yourself afterward.

This plan interrupts both. It keeps you from reliving, and it keeps you from escalating.

It also strengthens a deeper message:
"I can be triggered and still stay with myself."

That message is what creates durability. Not perfect calm. Self-trust under stress.

Over time, you will notice something changes. The same triggers happen, but the drop is less steep. The recovery is faster.

The moment feels more workable.
That isn't accidental.
That's you living without reopening.

Allowing Yourself to Be Ordinary

After survival, ordinariness can feel underwhelming.

No crisis.
No narrative arc.
No emotional intensity.

But ordinary is where stability lives.

It's where:

- Preferences emerge
- Trust rebuilds
- Life stops feeling like a test

You're allowed to want a life that doesn't require constant self-examination.

The End of Hyper-Explanation

Another sign of integration is the quiet end of explanation.

You stop:

- Justifying boundaries with backstory
- Explaining why certain things are hard
- Prefacing choices with context

You say no because no fits.
You leave because leaving feels right.
You stay because staying aligns.

Not everything requires a narrative.

That's not defensiveness. That's self-possession.

When You're Not Sure How to Describe Yourself Anymore

There's a moment many people experience during this phase.

Someone asks, *"So, tell me about yourself."*
And the old answers don't come.

Not because you don't have anything to say, but because you no longer define yourself by what you endured.

This can feel disorienting. But it's also a sign that your identity is no longer anchored to pain.

What comes next is quieter, and more honest.

Living Without a "Before and After"

Many people unconsciously divide their lives into:

- Before it happened
- After it happened

This framing gives the past enormous weight. Integration softens that divide.

You begin to think in terms of chapters instead of fractures.

Some chapters are intense.
Some are quiet.
Some are transitional.

Not every chapter needs to revolve around healing to be meaningful.

When Growth Stops Being Obvious

At this stage, growth may not *feel* like growth.

You're not constantly processing.
You're not tracking progress.
You're not working on yourself all the time.

You're just responding to life.

That's not stagnation. That's integration.

Letting the Past Be True Without Letting It Be Central

One of the most grounded positions you can take is this:
What happened to me is true, and it's not the most important thing about me anymore.

This doesn't minimize your experience. It contextualizes it.

You're not your hardest moment.
You're not your adaptations.
You're not your survival strategies.

Those were responses, not definitions.

When You Stop Checking Who You're "Supposed" to Be

As identity stabilizes, expectations soften.

You stop asking:

- *Should I be over this by now?*
- *Should I want something different?*
- *Should I be further along?*

You start asking:

- *What feels honest today?*
- *What feels sustainable?*

Those questions don't come from pain.
They come from presence.

The Quiet Confidence of Integration

Confidence after survival is rarely loud. It shows up as:

- Fewer explanations
- Slower decisions
- Clearer boundaries
- Less urgency
- More presence

You're no longer trying to prove anything, to yourself or to anyone else.

When Old Memories Appear, and You Stay Where You Are

Even now, the past may still visit.

A memory surfaces.
A feeling passes through.

The difference is that it no longer relocates you.

You stay in your body.
You stay in the present.
You stay in your life.

The memory moves through, not something you follow.

Identity as Something You Live, Not Explain

At this stage, identity isn't something you articulate easily.
It's something you embody.

You respond instead of react.
You choose without over-justifying.
You rest without guilt.
You move forward without rushing.

You don't need a name for this version of yourself.
You're already living it.

What This Chapter Asks of You

Not to reinvent yourself.
Not to declare a new identity.

Only this:

Let yourself be guided by who you are now, not who you had to become.

The past no longer needs to explain you. You're allowed to live without armor.

Where This Leaves You

Becoming someone who isn't defined by what hurt them doesn't mean rejecting your past.

It means releasing its authority.

You remember without reliving.
You feel without collapsing.
You choose without consulting history.

And that version of you, quiet, grounded, present, is not fragile.

They're free.

CHAPTER 8

REBUILDING TRUST IN YOURSELF AFTER LETTING GO

Letting go creates space.

And space, while necessary, can feel unexpectedly unsettling.

When the past loosens its grip, when the emotional charge fades and the constant referencing stops, many people expect to feel immediately confident. Certain. Grounded. Ready.

Instead, what often shows up first is hesitation.

You pause before decisions. You second-guess yourself. You feel unsure in moments that once felt obvious. This can be alarming.

After everything you've worked through, the last thing you expect is doubt.

And so, a new question emerges, quiet but persistent:

Can I trust myself now?
This question doesn't mean you're regressing.

It means you're transitioning.

Why Self-Trust Often Weakens Before It Strengthens

For a long time, your choices may have been organized around avoidance.

Avoiding pain.
Avoiding repetition.
Avoiding mistakes you couldn't afford to make again.

That structure, while heavy, provided orientation.

When you let go of the past, you also release the framework that once told you what *not* to do. And without that reference point, decision-making can feel exposed.

You're no longer reacting. You're choosing.

And choice requires a different kind of trust than survival ever did.

Self-Trust Isn't a Feeling, it's a Relationship

Most people think self-trust is something you either have or don't. It's not.

Self-trust is built the same way trust with anyone else is built, through experience.

You don't trust yourself because you tell yourself you should. You trust yourself because you see yourself respond, adjust, and recover.

Confidence comes later. Trust comes first.

How to Repair With Yourself After You Slip

One of the fastest ways to rebuild self-trust isn't by getting everything right.

It's by learning how to repair when you don't. Most people think self-trust is built through flawless decisions.

But self-trust is built through a different promise:
"I won't abandon myself when things get messy."

This matters because many people don't lose self-trust from one mistake. They lose it from what happens afterward.

They judge themselves. They spiral. They punish. They overcorrect. They rewrite the story as proof they can't be trusted.

So, it helps to learn a simple self-repair process. Not as therapy. As a way of staying in relationship with yourself.

STEP ONE: Name the slip without a sentence of shame

A slip could be anything.

You replied when you meant to pause. You checked something you promised yourself you would stop checking. You ignored your own boundary. You said yes out of pressure.

The first step is naming it plainly: "I slipped."

Not "I'm pathetic."
Not "I ruined everything."
Not "I never change."

Shame turns a moment into an identity.
Clarity keeps it as a moment.

STEP TWO: Identify the need underneath

Most slips are not random. They are attempts to meet a need.

A need for reassurance. A need for connection. A need for relief. A need for control. A need to avoid discomfort.

Ask: *"What was I needing in that moment?"*

This isn't an excuse. It's information.

When you understand the need, you can meet it differently next time.

STEP THREE: Offer yourself a repair statement

A repair statement is a short sentence that keeps you connected to yourself.

Examples:

"That makes sense. I was overwhelmed."
"I see why I did that. I was looking for relief."
"I can learn from this without punishing myself."

This isn't softness for softness' sake.

It's how you prevent the second injury, which is self-abandonment.

STEP FOUR: Make one small corrective action

Self-trust grows when you take a next step, even a small one.

- If you broke a boundary, reinforce it now.
- If you overexplained, stop explaining and rest.
- If you checked something, close it and do a present-time action.

The corrective action doesn't need to be perfect.
It needs to be real.

It teaches your system: "We can course-correct."

STEP FIVE: Update the plan, not your worth

Many people treat slips as proof. Proof they haven't changed.

But slips are data. So instead of collapsing into self-judgment, adjust one thing.

Examples:

- If fatigue increases slips, you need more rest, not more discipline
- If certain people trigger slips, you need stronger boundaries, not stronger willpower
- If uncertainty triggers checking, you need regulation tools, not more analysis

This turns the slip into progress.

Not because it feels good, but because it becomes useful.

Why repair builds trust faster than control

Control is fragile. It requires perfect conditions.

Repair is durable. It works even when conditions are imperfect.

When you learn to repair with yourself, you stop living with the fear that one misstep will undo you. That fear is what keeps many people stuck.

Self-trust grows when you know: *"I can handle it if I mess up."*

Not with panic. With repair.

A new definition of reliable

Reliable doesn't mean you'll never struggle. Reliable means you don't disappear from yourself when you do.

You return.
You respond.
You adjust.

That's the kind of trust that lasts. And it's built through moments exactly like these.

Not the perfect days. The messy ones where you choose to stay on your own side.

What Post-Healing Doubt Actually Looks Like

This phase is easy to misinterpret.

You may notice:

- Overthinking small decisions
- Wanting reassurance, you didn't need before
- Hesitating even when nothing feels wrong
- Fear of repeating yourself
- A sense of *I don't want to mess this up*

This isn't weakness. It's caution recalibrating.

Your system is learning how to operate without fear as its primary guide.

The Fear of Repeating Yourself

One of the biggest obstacles to self-trust is the fear of repetition.

You might think:

- *What if I miss the signs again?*
- *What if I end up back where I started?*
- *What if I haven't actually changed?*

These fears are understandable, but outdated.

You're not making decisions from the same awareness.
You're not ignoring the same signals.
You're not operating with the same capacity.

Growth doesn't make mistakes impossible. It makes recovery faster, and less catastrophic.

How Survival Undermines Trust Over Time

When survival is required, mistakes feel dangerous. They don't feel like learning experiences. They feel like threats.

So, your system learns:

- Double-check everything
- Delay commitment
- Scan for certainty
- Avoid irreversible choices

These strategies once kept you safe.

After letting go, they can quietly keep you stuck.

Over-caution looks like wisdom. Hesitation feels responsible.

But trust feels different. It feels steady, not tight.

Intuition vs. Fear Conditioning

One of the hardest parts of rebuilding self-trust is learning the difference between intuition and fear.

Fear speaks urgently.
It demands certainty.
It fixates on consequences.

Intuition is quieter.

It doesn't rush.
It doesn't argue.
It doesn't need proof.

After years of vigilance, intuition can feel unfamiliar, almost too subtle to trust.

But that subtlety is the point.

Fear shouts. Presence whispers.

Why Small Decisions Matter More Than Big Ones

Many people try to rebuild confidence by making big, symbolic choices. This often backfires.

Self-trust isn't restored through pressure. It's rebuilt through follow-through. Small, low-stakes decisions teach your system something crucial: *I listen to myself, and I respond accordingly.*

This might look like:

- Saying no when something feels off
- Leaving earlier than planned
- Resting instead of pushing
- Changing your mind without shame
- Choosing what feels aligned, not impressive

Each of these moments' deposits trust.

When Overthinking Is Actually Distrust

Overthinking often feels responsible. But underneath it's usually a lack of trust.

You think more because you don't believe your initial response is valid. You search for certainty because you don't trust your ability to respond if things go wrong.

Try asking yourself:
Am I seeking clarity, or avoiding trusting myself?

Sometimes the most self-trusting move is deciding without full certainty.

Learning to Decide Without the Past's Approval

As long as the past remains an authority, self-trust can't fully form.

You don't need to ask:

- *Does this prove I've learned?*
- *Would the old me approve?*
- *Is this safe according to what happened?*

Those questions keep you tethered.
Instead, try:

- *What feels honest right now?*
- *What allows me to stay present?*
- *What choice respects who I am today?*

Self-trust grows when the present gets a vote.

When Emotional Quiet Feels Like Disconnection

After letting go, emotions may feel less intense.

Signals feel softer. Reactions less dramatic.

This can feel like disconnection, but it's not. It's clarity without distortion.

For a long time, fear amplified everything. Without it, your inner world may feel calmer, and unfamiliar. Trust returns as you learn to listen at this new volume.

Self-Compassion Is the Backbone of Trust

You can't build trust in an environment of punishment. If you only trust yourself when things go well, you'll live defensively.

Self-trust sounds like:

- *I trust myself to notice when something feels wrong.*
- *I trust myself to adjust.*
- *I trust myself to take care of myself if I misstep.*

That's not resignation. That's resilience.

A Daily Question That Rebuilds Trust Naturally

At the end of the day, ask: *Where did I listen to myself today?* It might be something small.

Noticing these moments trains your focus away from mistakes and toward alignment. Trust grows where attention goes.

When Confidence Doesn't Look Like Boldness

Post-healing confidence is quiet. It looks like:

- Fewer explanations
- Slower decisions
- Clearer boundaries
- Less urgency
- More presence

You're no longer trying to prove competence. You're living it.

Trusting Your Pace

There's no deadline for certainty.

You don't need to rush into new identities, relationships, or life directions to validate your growth.

Movement at your own pace isn't stagnation.

It's discernment. Trust includes patience.

When You Stop Asking for Guarantees

Eventually, something shifts.

You stop demanding certainty before acting.
You stop waiting for perfect clarity.

You act, not recklessly, not fearfully, but *responsively*.
That's self-trust in motion.

What This Chapter Asks of You

Not to be fearless.
Not to be decisive all the time.

Only this: Notice whether you treat yourself as someone you trust, or someone you monitor.

Self-trust doesn't arrive all at once. It accumulates, quietly, every time you show up for yourself.

Where This Leaves You

Rebuilding trust in yourself doesn't mean doubt disappears.

It means doubt no longer stops you.

You trust yourself to:

- Feel uncertainty without freezing
- Make decisions without guarantees
- Respond rather than panic
- Adjust without self-punishment

You don't need the past to guide you anymore.
You have something steadier now.
You have yourself.

CHAPTER 9
LIVING BEYOND THE PAST WITHOUT LOSING YOURSELF

There's a moment in this process that's so quiet, it's easy to miss.

It doesn't feel like achievement.
It doesn't feel like resolution.
It doesn't even feel like healing.

It feels like *neutrality*.

You wake up one day and realize you didn't think about the past yesterday, not because you were avoiding it, but because it simply didn't come up. Or maybe it did, briefly, and then passed without pulling you under.

You don't feel proud of this. You just notice it.

And that noticing carries a subtle question: *Is this it?*

Not disappointment. Not confusion. Just recognition that something fundamental has shifted, and that the shift doesn't look the way you were taught to expect.

When Healing Stops Feeling Like Healing

For much of this journey, healing required effort.

You reflected.
You processed.
You noticed patterns.
You monitored reactions.

Healing was something you *did*.

But at some point, that effort begins to taper off, not because you've stopped caring, but because it's no longer required.

You stop tracking progress.
You stop asking whether you're *"over it."*
You stop checking whether you're doing this right.

This is often where people get uneasy. They mistake quiet for stagnation. They mistake neutrality for numbness.

But this isn't disconnection. It's integration.

Integration Is When the Past Stops Being the Reference Point

Integration doesn't erase what happened.
It changes where it lives.

The past moves from the center of your identity to the background of your experience. It becomes something you *know*, not something you consult.

You no longer ask:

- *What does this say about what happened?*
- *How does this compare to before?*
- *Am I repeating something?*

You ask:

- *What feels right now?*
- *What do I want to do today?*
- *What supports the life I'm living?*

That shift is subtle, but decisive.

Letting Go of the Healing Identity

One of the last things many people release, without realizing it, is the identity of being someone who is healing.

For a long time, that identity served you. It gave you language, permission, and structure. It helped you relate to pain without being consumed by it.

But staying in a healing identity for too long can quietly keep the past central.

At some point, healing stops being an identity and becomes a *context*.

You're no longer someone who is healing.
You're someone who is *living*.

When the Past Is Still True, but No Longer Central

There's a grounded emotional position that emerges at this stage:

What happened to me is true, and it's no longer the most important thing about me.

This doesn't minimize your experience. It doesn't deny its impact. It simply refuses to let pain be the organizing principle of your life.

You're not your hardest moment.
You're not your adaptations.
You're not the version of you who had to survive.

Those were responses, not definitions.

A Life That Is Not a Reaction

When the past is no longer the reference point, a new question becomes available.

Not *"What happened?"*
Not *"Why did it happen?"*
Not *"What does it mean about me?"*

A simpler question:
What do I want my life to be about now?

This can feel surprisingly hard to answer. Not because you lack imagination, but because reaction has been an organizing principle for so long.

When you're reacting, your life is shaped by what you're avoiding. When you're living, your life is shaped by what you're choosing.

That shift is quiet, but it's everything.

Reaction has a signature

A reaction-shaped life often includes:
Decisions made to prevent regret.

- Relationships managed to avoid conflict
- Goals chosen to prove you're okay
- Routines built around control
- A constant background sense of *"don't mess this up"*

None of this means you're doing life wrong. It means your system learned to prioritize safety.

But there's a difference between safety and aliveness.

Safety is necessary.
Aliveness is what makes the life worth inhabiting.

Choice isn't a grand reinvention

When people hear *"create a new life,"* they often picture dramatic change.

A move. A new relationship. A career shift. A complete personality makeover. But living beyond the past usually begins much smaller.

It begins with: *Saying what you actually want for dinner*

Resting without turning it into recovery. Taking a walk without using it to think. Buying something because you like it, not because it signals anything. Letting a good moment be good without scanning for the catch.

These choices seem minor.

But they teach your system:
"My present gets to lead."

A helpful distinction: values vs proof

A lot of people unknowingly build their lives around proof. Proof they are healed. Proof they are strong. Proof they are not naive. Proof they are over it. Proof is exhausting because it never ends.

Values are different. Values are what you live from, not what you perform.

A values-based life asks:
What matters to me even when no one is watching?

That question is often where identity starts to rebuild in a stable way. Not as a reaction to pain. As a return to what is true.

Three small anchors for a non-reaction life

If you're not sure what you want your life to be about, start with anchors rather than big answers. Here are three that often help.

- **Ease:** Not laziness. Ease. The willingness to stop making everything hard to prove you're capable.

- **Honesty:** The ability to name what's true in you today, without making it a case.

- **Enoughness:** The decision to stop treating peace as something you must earn.

These anchors don't require a new personality. They require a new permission.

Letting your life be bigger than your insight

Many people become very good at insight. They understand themselves deeply. They can name patterns quickly. They can see dynamics in real time.

That's valuable.

But if your life becomes a constant reflection exercise, you can end up living beside it rather than in it. A life beyond the past includes less commentary. More participation.

You stop asking yourself to narrate every feeling.
You let feelings come and go while you keep living.

This isn't avoidance. It's capacity.

When the old story tries to return as identity

Even late in this process, the old story may try to reassert itself. Not as pain, but as definition.

You may catch yourself thinking:

"This is just who I am now."
"I'm the kind of person who…"
"I can't because…"

Sometimes that's true. Sometimes it's just an old adaptation asking to remain in charge.

You don't have to argue with it.

You can simply ask:
Is that still true, or was it true in a season I have outgrown?

Outgrowing isn't betrayal. It's development.

A simple way to begin living forward

Choose one area of life where you want less reaction.

It could be:

- Your mornings
- Your phone use
- Your relationships
- How you respond to criticism
- How you spend your weekends

Then choose one small action that reflects who you're becoming. Not who you're proving. Who you're *becoming*.

Examples:

- If you want less reaction in relationships, practice pausing before replying
- If you want less reaction in your routines, schedule one hour with no productivity goal
- If you want less reaction in your self-talk, replace *"what's wrong with me?"* with *"what do I need?"*

This is how identity shifts. Through lived behavior. Not declarations.

The quiet payoff

When your life is no longer organized around what hurt you, you may not feel a dramatic victory.

You will feel something subtler.
You will feel less internal negotiation.

Less bracing.
Less self-monitoring.
More room.

Not because the past vanished, but because it stopped being your compass. That's the real outcome.

A life that's not a reaction. A life that belongs to *you*.

And you don't have to announce it. You just keep choosing it, one ordinary day at a time.

Living Without a "Before and After"

Many people unconsciously divide their lives into two parts:

Before it happened.
After it happened.

This framing gives the past enormous gravity. Everything else becomes a reaction to it.

Integration softens this divide. You begin to think in terms of chapters instead of fractures.

Some chapters are intense.
Some are quiet.
Some are transitional.

Not every chapter needs to justify itself by referencing pain. Your life doesn't need to orbit what hurt you.

When You Stop Explaining Yourself

One of the quiet signs that the past no longer defines you is that you explain yourself less.

You don't preface choices with backstory.
You don't justify boundaries with history.
You don't narrate your growth.

You say no because no fits.
You leave because leaving feels right.
You stay because staying aligns.

This isn't secrecy. It's self-possession.

Identity Without Armor

For a long time, your identity may have included protection.

Being careful.
Being alert.
Being prepared.

Those traits once kept you safe.

As they soften, you may feel strangely exposed at first, like you're missing something important.

What you're missing isn't protection. It's armor.

And armor is heavy. Living without it doesn't make you vulnerable. It makes you responsive.

When Ordinary Life Becomes Enough

After survival, many people expect life to feel extraordinary.

But integration often brings something else:

- Ordinary days that don't require emotional management.
- Conversations that don't need internal monitoring.
- Calm moments that don't feel suspicious.

This can feel underwhelming if you're used to intensity.

But ordinariness is where *stability* lives.

It's where preferences form.
Where trust rebuilds naturally.
Where your nervous system rests.

You're allowed to want a life that doesn't feel like a test.

When Old Memories Appear, and You Stay Where You Are

Even now, memories may still surface.

A thought drifts through.
A feeling passes briefly.

The difference is that you don't relocate.

You don't step into the memory.
You don't follow the story.
You don't brace for impact.

You stay here, in your body, in the present, in your life. The memory moves through instead of pulling you back.

That's not avoidance. That's completion.

The End of Measuring Yourself Against the Past

Another quiet shift happens when you stop comparing yourself to earlier versions of you.

You're no longer trying to prove you've grown.
You're no longer correcting old mistakes retroactively.
You're no longer measuring progress by distance from pain.

You're simply responding to what's in front of you.

That's not stagnation. That's presence.

Choosing Without Consultation

At this stage, decisions come from a different place.

- You don't consult the past.
- You don't check whether a choice aligns with your healing narrative.
- You don't ask whether this proves anything.

You choose based on *alignment*.

Not excitement. Not fear. Alignment.

It feels steady. Unforced. Quietly right.

When Peace Stops Being Fragile

Earlier, peace may have felt conditional.

You waited for it to break.
You watched it closely.
You expected interruption.

Now, peace feels neutral.

Not something to protect.
Not something to maintain.

Just available.

You stop asking what's wrong when nothing is happening.

Living Without Needing Meaning

There's often pressure to extract meaning from pain.

A lesson.
A transformation.
A reason it all happened.

But not all experiences resolve neatly.

Sometimes the most honest thing you can do is stop trying to make sense of it, and start making room for what's next.

Your life doesn't need to justify itself. It only needs to be lived.

The Quiet Confidence That Replaces Control

Confidence at this stage doesn't look like certainty.
It looks like trust.

Trust that:

- *You can* feel discomfort without collapsing
- *You can* make decisions without guarantees
- *You can* adjust without self-punishment
- *You can* live without constant self-reference

This trust isn't loud. It's stable.

When You Stop Asking, "Am I Healed?"

Eventually, the question itself loses relevance. Not because everything is resolved, but because it no longer matters.

You're not measuring your life by proximity to pain anymore. You're participating in it. That's the quiet end of healing.

What This Chapter Asks of You

Nothing new. No action. No commitment. No promise.
Only *permission*.

Permission to stop organizing your life around what hurt you. Permission to live without constant self-evaluation. Permission to let this be enough.

You don't need to keep proving that you've let go. You don't need to arrive anywhere else.

Where This Leaves You

Letting go doesn't mean the past disappears. It means it stops driving. You keep the wisdom. You release the weight.

And you move forward, not as someone defined by what hurt them, but as someone capable of living beyond it.

Not dramatically. Not loudly.

But *fully*.

A TWO-WEEK LETTING-GO RESET

DAILY PROMPTS TO LOOSEN THE GRIP GENTLY

This isn't a challenge. It's not a program. It's not a test of how well you understood this book.

And it's not something you need to complete perfectly, or at all, to have benefited from what you've read.

Think of this reset as a quiet companion.

Something you return to when you notice the past creeping closer than you'd like. Something you move through slowly, skip around in, or revisit months from now when life tightens again.

Nothing here is meant to fix you. It's meant to **create space**.

How to Use This Reset (Without Turning It Into Work)

You don't need a journal, a schedule, or uninterrupted time.

You can:

- Read a prompt in the morning and think about it later

- Sit with one prompt for several days

- Skip days that don't resonate

- Return only when you need grounding

This reset works best when approached with curiosity instead of discipline.

If anything, here feels heavy, that's information, not failure.

You're allowed to pause.

WEEK ONE
Creating Distance Without Resistance

The first week isn't about release.
It's about *distance*.

Before you let go of anything, your system needs to learn that closeness is optional. That you can notice the past without stepping into it. That you can feel something old without reopening the story.

Nothing more is required.

Day 1
What Are You Still Carrying Without Realizing It?

Today is about noticing, not solving.

Ask yourself:

- What thoughts come up most often when I'm tired or quiet?
- What situations still tighten me internally, even if I function through them?
- What feels "normal" to carry that actually costs me energy?

You're not looking for action. You're identifying what's still traveling with you.

Awareness is the first form of distance.

Day 2
When the Past Shows Up, How Close Does It Get?

Notice proximity today.

When something from the past arises:

- Do you step into it emotionally?
- Do you analyze it?
- Do you feel pulled backward?

Or do you notice it and stay where you are? There is no right response.

Just notice how close the past gets, and how quickly.

Day 3
What Do You Automatically Brace For?

Bracing is often invisible until you look for it.

Notice moments when you:

- Prepare explanations in advance
- Tighten before speaking
- Expect misunderstanding or disappointment
- Hold back without knowing why

Ask gently:
What am I preparing for right now?

Often, the answer belongs to the past, not the present.

Day 4
What Would It Mean to Not Engage Today?

Choose one small moment today where you don't engage with an old pattern.

This might mean:

- Not replaying a conversation
- Not mentally defending yourself
- Not revisiting a familiar thought loop

You're not suppressing anything.
You're experimenting with non-participation.

Day 5
What Has This Pain Already Taught You?

Today is about honoring without carrying.

Ask:

- What lessons from this experience do I already understand?

- What insights no longer need reinforcement?

Some learning is complete.

You don't need to keep reviewing a lesson you've integrated.

Day 6
What Do You No Longer Need to Prove?

Pain is often carried as proof.

Proof that:

- It mattered
- You were affected
- You changed

Ask: *What am I still proving by holding onto this?*

Then ask: *Who am I proving it to?*

Often, no one is still watching.

Day 7
How Does Distance Feel in Your Body?

Notice how your body responds when you don't engage.

Do you feel:

- Relief?
- Guilt?
- Emptiness?
- Discomfort?

All responses are valid.

Distance doesn't always feel good at first. It feels unfamiliar. And unfamiliar isn't unsafe.

WEEK TWO
Reclaiming the Present Without Pressure

The second week isn't about becoming someone new.

It's about inhabiting where you are now, without referencing what hurt you.

Day 8
What Does the Present Ask of You Today?

Instead of asking what you *should* do

Ask: *What does today actually need?*

This might be:

- Rest
- Simplicity
- Honesty
- Slowness

Presence begins when you respond to what's real.

Day 9
What Feels Aligned Without Explanation?

Notice what feels right without justification.

This might look like:

- Saying no
- Leaving early
- Wanting something small
- Changing your mind

Alignment doesn't argue.

It just is.

Day 10
Where Are You Still Seeking Permission?

Ask yourself:

- Where am I waiting for approval?
- Whose understanding am I hoping for?

Permission-seeking often keeps the past relevant.

Notice where you can quietly grant yourself permission instead.

Day 11
What Does Trust Look Like in Small Moments?

Self-trust isn't built through big decisions.

Notice moments where you:

- Listen to your body
- Respect a boundary
- Respond instead of react

Trust grows through consistency, not certainty.

Day 12
What Are You Allowed to Enjoy Now?

Pain often limits pleasure long after it's gone.

Ask: *What am I allowed to enjoy without earning it?*

Let enjoyment be simple.

No meaning required.

Day 13
Who Are You Without the Story Today?

For one day, notice who you are when you don't reference the past.

How do you:

- Speak
- Choose
- Move through the day

This isn't denial.

It's presence.

Day 14
What Can You Put Down Gently?

Ask: *What can I stop carrying, not forever, just for now?*

Let it be small.
Let it be kind.
Let it be enough.

A Note About Returning to This Reset

You may return to this reset many times.

Not because you failed, but because life changes.

Stress tightens old patterns.
Transitions bring old material forward.

Returning here doesn't mean you're back at the beginning.

It means you know where to land.

What This Bonus Is Meant to Leave You With

Not discipline.
Not vigilance.
Not responsibility for staying healed.

Just *familiarity*.

With distance.
With presence.
With choice.

You don't need to hold onto what already taught you what it could.

You're allowed to live forward, gently, imperfectly, and without pressure.

EPILOGUE

If You Find Yourself Back Here

At some point after finishing this book, the past may visit again.

Not dramatically. Not in a way that means anything is wrong. It might show up as a thought you didn't expect, a feeling you haven't had in a while, or a moment where something old feels closer than it has recently.

When that happens, it can be tempting to assume you've gone backward.

You haven't.

Letting go isn't a one-time event. It's a relationship that changes as you do.

When Old Things Return

There will be seasons when distance feels natural and effortless.

There may also be moments, often during stress, transition, fatigue, or change, when old material briefly resurfaces. This doesn't undo your progress.

It simply means your nervous system remembers what once mattered.

What's different now isn't the absence of memory.

It's your response.

You no longer have to:

- Re-enter the story
- Analyze what already taught you enough
- Treat the past as unfinished business

You can notice, acknowledge, and return to where you are.

That isn't failure.
That's integration.

If You Revisit This Book

You may find yourself returning to parts of this book, not because you need to relearn anything, but because certain words land differently at different times.

Re-reading isn't a sign that you missed something. It's a sign that you've changed.

Nothing here is meant to be "maintained."

You aren't responsible for holding a healed version of yourself together.

Healing that lasts is quiet, adaptable, and forgiving of fluctuation.

What Progress Really Looks Like

If you ever wonder whether you've truly moved on, notice this:

- You recover faster.
- You stay present more easily.
- You don't get pulled as far.
- You don't stay as long.

That's not accidental.
That's the work living inside you.

You Don't Need a Permanent State

You may never reach a point where the past feels completely irrelevant.

But you can reach a point where it no longer interrupts your life.

- *You don't* need to close every loop.
- *You don't* need to resolve every feeling.
- *You don't* need to be certain you're done.

You only need to keep choosing the present when you notice yourself drifting backward.

And even when you don't choose it perfectly, you still return.

That's the difference now.

You're Allowed to Stop Carrying This

This book doesn't ask you to carry anything forward except permission.

- Permission to stop holding what already taught you what it could.
- Permission to live without constant self-reference.
- Permission to trust that you don't need to revisit the past to honor it.

- *You're allowed* to live a life that isn't organized around what hurt you.
- *You're allowed* to feel peace without waiting for it to be taken away.
- And *you're allowed* to let this be enough.

Closing

You don't need to do anything with what you've read.
You don't need to apply it perfectly.
You don't need to remember every word.

What matters is that something shifted. The past no longer sits in the driver's seat.

And you don't need to announce that.

You just live from here.

ACKNOWLEDGMENTS

First, to anyone who picked this up because something in you is tired of carrying what you already survived. If you've been functioning but not free, this book is for you.

Thank you to the people who keep showing up for their own healing, even when it's slow, messy, and quiet. The ones who keep choosing the next honest step instead of the dramatic one. The ones who don't post about it, don't perform it, and still do it.

Thank you to the friends, partners, and family members who make room for change. The ones who don't demand the old version of someone just because it's familiar. The ones who listen without fixing, and stay without needing the story to be simple.

Thank you to the helpers who do this work with care. The therapists, counselors, coaches, clinicians, support workers, and steady professionals who treat the nervous system like it's allowed to learn a new way. The ones who take pain seriously, without making it permanent.

Thank you to every person who has ever said some version of, *"I know it's over, so why does it still feel like this?"* Your honesty shaped the heart of these pages. The details are not yours, but the truth is real.

And finally, thank you to the reader who isn't trying to become a brand-new person. You're just trying to come back to yourself. That is more than enough.

What Do I Do Next?

If you finished this book and thought, *"Okay, I understand myself better, but how do I actually live this,"* here are a few options.

1. **Re-read the chapter that hit you hardest**
   Not the chapter you liked most, the one that made you pause. The one that made you feel exposed. Go back and choose one small practice from that chapter to try for seven days.

2. **Start a simple "grip log"**
   Not to overanalyze. Just to notice patterns. When does the past tighten in your body, your thoughts, or your behavior. What sets it off. What you do next. Awareness without judgment is how the grip starts to loosen.

3. **Pick one relationship and soften one habit**
   Not a big confrontation. Something quiet and practical. Maybe you stop overexplaining. Maybe you do not rehearse the conversation. Maybe you leave one message unanswered until you feel settled. Small changes teach your system what safety feels like now.

4. **Use the Two-Week Reset the way it's meant to be used**
   One day at a time. No catching up. No doing it perfectly. If a day doesn't fit your situation, adapt it. The point is practice, not performance.

Whatever you do next, don't confuse familiarity with truth. Just because your system still reacts doesn't mean you're back where you started. Keep choosing the next small thing that returns you to yourself.

ABOUT THE AUTHOR

Amelia Oliver-Lilly writes reader-first nonfiction for people who want practical clarity, not perfect-life advice. Her books are made for real life: plain-English guidance, simple frameworks, and tools you can use when you're short on time, energy, or patience. No fluff, no lectures, and no "just manifest it" nonsense.

Let Go Without Losing Yourself is for anyone who has moved on in the obvious ways, but still feels the grip in the quiet ones: the overthinking, the bracing, the lingering pull of old patterns. Amelia's approach is not about forcing closure or becoming a new person. It's about loosening what survival taught you, without abandoning who you are.

If this book helped you feel a little more like yourself again, the best thank you is to pass it on to someone who's carrying more than they admit.

9 781764 573917